CRIPPLE

CRIPPLE

The Story of an American Journey

JERRY A. RANGE

To order additional copies of this book, contact:
Xlibris Corporation
1-888-795-4274
www.Xlibris.com
Orders@Xlibris.com
23950

CONTENTS

This is for Jeannie,
who always has loved me unconditionally.
Without Jeannie the story of my life would
not have been worth the telling . . .

INTRODUCTION

There is no instruction manual that comes with the crippling of a human being. In addition to that, some people are better suited to deal with a severe physical handicap than others.

While on paper that may seem obvious, most able-bodied people would be hard put to look at a number of handicapped people and determine which ones are at peace with their lot in life and which ones have warfare roaring inside their minds and hearts.

If God had intended people to be seriously crippled, He should have provided them with personalities that would make it easy for them to deal with the never-ending frustrations, large and small, that fill the days of someone who is seriously handicapped.

I do not care about political correctness in language. Specifically, in regards to the subject of this true story—me—I will simply say that there is no particular concern on my part for language describing someone with a severe physical handicap.

As I understand it, the present politically correct term is "physically challenged." Frankly, I think "crippled," "handicapped," or "physically disabled" come closer to the mark.

There have been many books written about people who have overcome serious physical handicaps and who have gone on to do great things. Many of those people will say that they have conquered the frustrations of being crippled.

I can honestly say that every day when I awake, the battle with frustration begins anew.

My goal always was achieving normalcy.

Just trying to be normal on a daily basis burned up an enormous amount of physical and emotional energy. The physical exertion was apparent to any casual observer. The burning away of emotional reserves was far less obvious. In my case, the bill came due as I entered my middle aged years.

There are people to whom I simply must say, "Thank you." They are people who made it possible for me to be a productive member of society, or as it is more commonly called, a "taxpayer."

Obviously, it begins with Mom and Dad. My father, the late W. L. "Pete" Range, and my mother, Mary Agnes Range, never let me think that I could not succeed in life. Particularly, they encouraged me to think that I would attend a college or university. Back in the early 1960s, that was no small hope for a severely crippled person.

It was my mother who always told me, "You should write a book." Well, Mom, here is that book.

The late Coach Art Teynor, my mentor in high school and my friend for life until his death from complications from diabetes in 1995, ranks high on my list of people to thank. He was a motivator, a great teacher, and a man who made me feel that I was valuable and useful. To do that, he made me feel that I was a part of his teams at old Dover (Ohio) St. Joseph High School.

There is an enormous debt that I can never repay to the staff of the Georgia Warm Springs Foundation in the late 1950s. Three names come to mind: physical therapist Charlotte "Bambi" Cranmore (her maiden name); director of physical therapy Ann Martin, and psychologist Grace Marie Freyman. Miss Freyman saw something in me that I did not know was there.

Many people deserve mention at the University of Illinois, which was the only university in the country in 1962 that recruited physically handicapped students.

That was long before the civil rights movement, which had a spill-over affect that nudged state governments into accommodating their own handicapped students. And it was long before the ADA (Americans with Disabilities Act).

(I am not so sure that I like the idea of the government forcing institutions to accept handicapped students. But that is fuel for another argument at another time).

This is the place to honor people who helped me.

There was Dr. Timothy Nugent, world-renowned pioneer in physical rehabilitation and a great student of human nature. There was his assistant, Joe Konitzky, one of the gentlest and kindest people I have ever known.

Dr. Nugent knew just which buttons to push in order to motivate a student. He did that for me at a critical time in my life.

Joe Konitzky's door was always open to any student who needed advice or a shoulder to cry on. Joe was the Father Confessor for many of us. Many of us loved him.

There are many professors who treated me with dignity and encouraged me to get a good liberal arts education.

Three come to mind immediately: Glenn Hanson, my adviser and a journalism professor who was responsible for the only two C's that I got in college. I never let him forget it. But his office was always open—as was his heart—and for 10 cents a student could get a cup of coffee and a large piece of the good professor's time.

There was Jay Jensen, director of the newspaper journalism program at Illinois. Dr. Jensen taught me, among other things, the significance of the word "weltenschauung." He also helped me get my first job, as a copy editor at the "Plain Dealer" in Cleveland.

Finally, there was Gene Graham, a Pulitzer Prize-winning journalist from Nashville, Tenn. Graham came to be a professor at Illinois by way of a Nieman Fellowship at Harvard University. He steered me toward newspaper journalism. He later became a close friend.

He was a great bear of a man with an unruly shock of red hair, and a southern drawl that camouflaged an enormous intellect. His body always seemed to be at war with his ill-fitting suits. He died of a massive brain tumor in the late 1970s. It seemed to be a terrible waste of a great mind and a good heart.

In my newspaper "career" of being a copy editor for 24 years, there are so many people that stand out that I would be slighting someone if I were to mention names. Suffice it to say, from the weird to the wonderful, their names are many.

I also want to include Eric Kennedy of Cleveland, the best damned lawyer in these United States.

Finally, there is Jeannie. Our union produced Michelle, Jerry Jr., Mary Rose, Christopher, Peter, and Patrick. Jeannie is primarily responsible for them being the magnificent young men and women that they have become.

In 34 years of marriage, I often made life difficult for her.

Nevertheless, Jeannie has taught me the meaning of self-sacrifice and of selfless love. She has enriched my life beyond my wildest dreams. Without her, I would be nothing. With her, I am made whole.

—Jerry A. Range, New Philadelphia, Ohio, 2004 A.D.

CHAPTER 1

"Into the Valley of Death"

Peter never saw it coming. The concussion, that is. He did not have the slightest notion that his brain was about to be rattled by a savage hit from a 6-foot-4, 250-pound defensive tackle for the Ridgewood High School team.

Peter, then 16, fifth of my six children and third of four sons, was 5-foot-9, and 160 pounds. He was quarterback for the "Saints" of little Tuscarawas Central Catholic High School in New Philadelphia, Ohio, in 1998. He was playing with a broken rib on his right side.

Week after week, knowing he was going to take a pounding, Peter went back onto the turf confident that he could push, pull, or drag a woebegone football team to a victory. In 1998, the Saints were 3-7. In 1999, only 19 players reported for preseason practice. The record was 1-9. The losses were huge: 56-0, 62-7, 55-0 being the norm.

Still, even while nursing another broken rib, Peter plugged away until the whistle ending the 10th and final game in 1999, a 59-7 physical and mental beating by a state powerhouse.

Week after week before leaving for school to suit up in the black and gold with the treasured fleur d'lis on his helmet, he would lean down to me in my wheelchair, give me a hug, and say something like, "We're going to it do it this week, Dad."

We were holding our own his junior year against Ridgewood, a big, tough, and experienced team. The score in the second quarter was 7-7, a surprise to everyone in the stadium. Peter was running to his left intending to throw to a receiver on the left sideline.

Sitting in the end zone some 35 yards away, I could see the huge lineman bearing down upon Peter. I was powerless to prevent the mayhem about to explode all over my son. Peter cocked his right arm. Before he could let the ball fly, the mammoth player slammed into him at full speed.

Like a rag doll being shaken in the mouth of a dog, Peter's small body went forward while his head snapped back. The aggressor slammed Peter into the turf and fell on him. The ball skittered away into the hands of the enemy, while their fans hooted and hollered in glee at the great "hit."

"Will Peter get up?" I wondered. Rubbery-legged, he was helped off the field. Ridgewood quickly scored. The rout was on.

After one game off, Peter was back at quarterback. Blindsided again and again on the gridiron, he would pick himself up, dust himself off, and go back at it.

That's how it was for me between my truncated childhood and my ascent through an adolescence and young adulthood as bizarre in its own way as an Alfred Hitchcock script.

Over and over again after being severely crippled by polio in all four limbs, I was urged to keep pushing, to keep working, to keep striving for success and if one battle was lost, then get up, go on, and win the next one.

The problem was that no one in all my rehabilitation ever defined what "success" ultimately would be. That would come back to haunt me when I was in my early 50s, at least four decades after I was blindsided in my own explosive confrontation with one of life's nastier situations.

My childhood died on Aug. 15, 1955.

Heralding its death was the mother of all headaches and a stabbing pain in my back.

The polio viruses which had been reproducing at a ferocious rate in my central nervous system for a week or 10 days made their presence known as my mother and I walked home from Mass on the Catholic feast day of the Assumption. Aug. 15 was also my mother's birthday. My father had left that day for a small town in Ohio to begin work as branch manager in a bottled gas outlet— his long awaited promotion.

With each step closer to our home in Erie, Pa., on that humid evening, fate was twisting tighter and tighter the lock on the door to a sparkling 11 years of boyhood.

Ahead lay a gray tunnel of pain, fear and uncertainty.

As we reached home, the twin pains were beating me down. When I asked my mother if I could go to bed early, my smart-aleck 13-year-old brother said, "He must be sick if he wants to go to bed."

Those were the days when general practitioners still made house calls. Our doctor examined me in the morning, noting the high fever and the twin pains familiar to family practitioners of the time. After talking with my mother beyond earshot of me, he said that we were going to take a little ride together to the hospital. Not to worry though, things would be just fine.

That is when my jaundiced view of doctors began.

As I walked down the front steps of our home, my beagle Skipper shot across my path.

"See you soon, Skip," I called.

He was too intent on picking up the scent of a rabbit to notice those final words of boyhood innocence or to see the final steps of a previously carefree boy.

━ ━ ━ ━ ━ ━ ━ ━ ━ ━

Hospitals are not user-friendly. These days they make a public-relations pretense of being nice places. The patina of false cheeriness gives faint hope to some. For someone like me, who has done time in 12 different hospitals, the key thing is just to get out alive.

In the mid-1950s, business was brisk in the contagion wards.

Poliomyelitis enjoyed a banner year in 1955, killing thousands, and crippling in varying degrees at least 65,000 other people. Maybe the evil microbes sensed their end was at hand, because the

Salk vaccine had been announced a year earlier and was being introduced in school inoculations. Perhaps, they intensified their efforts in 1955, knowing their malignant fun would soon end.

Whatever the reason, they went on a rampage.

Jerry Range, 11; inept Little Leaguer, missed his inoculation by about three weeks. It was a hard fate for a well-adjusted child of stern, but loving parents. Nevertheless, the second-fastest boy at Jefferson Elementary School unwittingly played generous host to the ravenous little bastards.

They gorged on my anterior horn cells, the messengers that carry orders from the brain out to the cells in muscle tissue.

The doctor told my mother on that golden-soft August morning that had been dipped in honey-sweet, late-summer sunshine that Jerry's case would be a mild one.

By "mild," he apparently meant two weeks of a fever hovering above 104 degrees, a month of unstoppable pain, and total paralysis, and thus unusable arms and legs.

It was a judgment call. Anyone can make minor miscalculations, even doctors; or maybe more accurately, especially doctors.

That first night in the hospital was unique for me, because it was the first night during which I did not sleep. I had never had a totally sleepless night before.

It was the first of what would be thousands of lonely nights spread across 48 years of being severely handicapped.

There is a special desperation known only by insomniacs. That night amid the merciless pain, fear, and loneliness, I paid my dues and joined the desperate fraternity.

— — — — — — — — —

My parents were that rare kind of couple that made heads wag and tongues cluck when they married in 1941. Theirs was what was known then as a "mixed" marriage—she was Catholic; he was Protestant.

Not only was that a strike against them, but almost as bad was that she was city-born and bred, while he was a product of a farm family that scratched out a life in the mountains along the far northern reaches of Pennsylvania's Allegheny River.

As an only child, Mary Agnes Nocera knew the creature comforts of a bustling city. While her parents, second generation Irish woman and second generation Italian man, were poor, she was an only child (a younger brother, for whom I was named, died at 7 of appendicitis).

She was doted on by well-to-do maiden aunts. She was a quick study in Catholic elementary school. At the city's largest and most prestigious public high school, Erie Academy, the pretty Mary Agnes had many potential beaus from well-placed families. She was editor of the school's yearbook.

Her future husband was one of seven children, six boys and one girl, born to a hard-working, stern mother of German descent, and a farmer-father of Huguenot ancestry. My grandfather supplemented the farm family's meager income by working in one of the many sawmills that clung to the mountainsides and dotted the hollows of Forest County.

Since her parents forbade her from attending college, the young Mary Agnes went through a short post-graduate business course, and then landed a job with the local phone company. She continued to live at home, as decent young women were expected to do in the 1930s. There her mother, a bit of a nag, could keep an eye on her.

The young woman chafed under such close scrutiny, but she endured it. Into her safe, but stifling world would saunter young, almost rakishly handsome Pete Range.

For a brief period after high school in East Hickory, young Range had stayed at the family farm while trying manual-labor. First he tried the sawmill, then farming, then the Works Project Administration, which was the effort by the Depression-era Roosevelt administration to create jobs with massive public construction efforts. Range worked on a crew hauling rocks up a hillside where a dam was planned.

He had too good a mind to continue at such labor for the WPA, which was ridiculed unfairly by critics as standing for "We Poke Along."

He said damn the dam, bade his worried parents goodbye and hitched a ride to the nearest city, Erie.

Raised a Free Methodist by his devout father, he converted to Lutheranism to play on the church softball team in Erie and qualify for free meals on weekends during summer softball season.

He found work in a casket factory, but he said that dead-end job was short-lived. Nearing the end of his meager savings, he lived on coffee and doughnuts for three days.

Strolling behind his boarding house and trying to figure out how to get his next meal, he saw the curvaceous, long-haired brunette Mary Nocera picking flowers in a yard nearby.

He forgot the growling in his stomach and walked toward the pretty young woman. Their courtship lasted four years, a not uncommon length in the cash-short Depression era. It was marked by hellacious scoldings by her mother and father.

Despite their threats of eviction, she continued seeing young Range. Then on a heart-crushing afternoon, her normally docile father, at the prodding of her mother, threw her out of the house.

Flush with money from his job as a truck driver for a local brewery, her fiance was dining on a large hamburger with fried potatoes—for 15 cents—when she burst sobbing through the doors of their favorite beanery, a gathering spot for young people in Erie. It was across the intersection from Veterans Memorial Stadium below her high-school alma mater.

Telling her to come with him, he headed straight for her house and was confronted by her father, who ordered him to leave.

"I won't leave until I get Mary's clothes, and if you don't get them for me, I'm coming in to get them myself," the brazen young man said. At six-foot, and with about 180 pounds hardened by manual labor, he was an imposing figure.

Her father threw her clothes into the front yard. She stayed at the house of a girl friend until they were able to marry. He signed the noxious pledge, then demanded in marriages between Catholics and non-Catholics. It was a document written in demeaning tones requiring that any children be raised as practicing Catholics.

The couple was not allowed to be married inside the sanctuary of the church. They were married Jan. 18, 1941, in the sacristy, a room to the side of the altar.

No relatives attended. Mary's good friend and her beau stood up for the gritty couple.

Two sons were rather quick results of the union. Tom arrived in January 1942. I hit the beach on June 9, 1944, three days after D-Day in Europe. While the rest of the world was anxiously awaiting the results of the Allied landing on Normandy's bloody apron, I was screaming for mother's milk.

Timing always has been one of my problems.

Aside from their perilous attraction for one another, the thing that young Pete Range and his bride had in common was ambition.

He had been in a hurry to leave behind the dirt-poor world of farming, sawmills, and WPA projects. He wanted very much to enter the white-collar world, where people used their minds instead of their stooped backs and calloused hands to make money.

For her part, Mary Agnes had felt cheated by her parents' refusal to let her enter college, even though scholarship aid was available. That disappointment would give birth to a constant theme in her upbringing of her three sons. (Jim was born in 1951).

There never was any question her sons would attend college. It was the typical, albeit vicarious, playing out of the American Dream—if she could not go to college and enter a profession, then her sons would.

Her doting aunts were a bit agitated by her marriage to a mountain-country Protestant, but they stayed supportive of their favorite niece.

With money from them, the little family moved out of a rental duplex to a neighborhood so perfect for young boys that it could have served as the set for Mickey Rooney's "Andy Hardy" series.

My 11 years at 301 Gridley Avenue are a golden memory, a place in my mind where in the next 48 years I could always return at times of high stress to draw on the golden reserves.

There was a city-owned forest behind the house. There was little car traffic. There was a creek nearby to play in during the summer and skate on during the long Erie winters. There was a large hill perfect for sled riding, and nearby was a city zoo and a park where former high school stars with beer bellies played semi-pro baseball.

Finally, and best of all, the neighborhood teemed with young boys.

What more could a boy ask?

In the three times when I have been treated for clinical depression, I have always told the psychologists and psychiatrists that I have no traumatic or disturbing memories from my childhood, before polio.

Certainly there are unpleasant ones, but nothing that tears at my heart.

I was a pleasant boy, so I have been told. Even though there was plenty to do out of doors, reading occupied much of my time. I was diligent in school, dutiful about my chores and loyal to my parents. At times, that proved a difficult balancing act, because my mother and father argued frequently over religion. She wanted me in Catholic schools, he insisted upon public grade schools.

During one row, he was slamming a rug, hung over a clothesline. He was talking of my mother and calling her "a son of a bitch," a phrase with which I was not yet familiar at five years of age. I trudged upstairs and saw my mother lying on their bed, crying. She asked me what my father had said, and innocently I told her. She sobbed louder. I went back downstairs and out to my father. He said, "What did your mother say about what I called her?" When I told him, he said to the open air, "She ought to be crying."

Whatever the issue was, their marriage survived for nearly 50 more years.

———————————

The Heinie incident indicates how dutiful, and dumb, a child I was. I had a paper route of about 80 customers. At one house, the family's German shepherd had been so abused and taunted by the previous paperboys, a family of hell-raising Irish lads, that he saw any paperboy as his mortal foe.

The dog was called Heine, and I was No. 1 on Heinie's hit list.

The family requested that their paper be placed on the front porch. The problem was that the canny, revenge-minded Heinie would lie in wait for me, often lunging and snarling at me.

Every day, I worried about how I would get the folded paper onto the porch. When Heinie would run around back, I would rush to the porch.

Sometimes our elaborate cat-and-mouse games would last 15 or 20 minutes. It never occurred to dumb and dutiful Jerry Range to just drop the paper on the lawn, or simply not deliver it at all.

Certainly, the "Erie Daily Times" wanted its customers well-served, but not at the risk of life and limb, particularly given the necessity of carrying liability insurance. A chunk of limb was what Heinie got one summer's day in 1955.

As I arrived in front of the house and dismounted from my bike, Heine was at the right corner of the porch, lying in the grass in the attack mode. I pondered how to get the paper to the porch and return alive.

As luck would have it, a bread truck arrived. The deliveryman and I exchanged pleasantries. "Nice day," he said. "Sure is," I answered, thinking all the while, "hurry up and carry your load of bread to the house." When he finally headed up the walk, I jumped to his left, keeping him between me and Heinie.

When we reached the mid-way point to the house, Heinie launched his attack with a savage snarl. "Now!," he must have been thinking, "now I get my revenge for those years of taunting by the humans who bring that tasteless object to my house every day!"

Heinie never had seemed interested in peaceful dialogue to work out a mutually acceptable accord. He was more action-oriented.

The snarling, gray-black blur reached my left knee in world-class time. My Levis were no match for his fangs. Both a sizable chunk of denim and flesh were gone before I knew what had hit me.

Seeing the blood gushing from the wound, the deliveryman said what seemed even to a boy of 11 a masterpiece of understatement.

"Gee, kid," he said, "he really got you good."

He rang the doorbell, and explained the situation to the lady of the house, asked if she wanted extra cinnamon buns that week, took her open-mouthed silence for a negative, and left. She took me inside, sat me on a chair near the front door and brought a cold compress, all the while probably wondering if the blood stains would come out of the carpet.

She went to the back of the house to telephone her husband, a doctor. No doubt while discussing whether they would be facing a lawsuit, the unthinking twit let the dog in the back door. I looked up from my teary-eyed examination of the garish wound to see Heinie poke his head around a wall, and start to growl.

As I began to stand and feel for the door handle, never taking my eyes off Heinie, the woman came back into the room and saw my discomfiture. She thoughtlessly blurted out a dog owner's most-practiced cliche: "Don't worry, he won't hurt you."

It was then that I discovered irony.

The rest of the tale of the revenge-minded dog and the dutifully dumb paperboy is unremarkable, except for one detail. The woman had phoned my father after calling her doctor-husband. At the emergency room of St. Vincent Hospital, her husband was studying the wound with another doctor when Dad arrived.

His words, snarled at the dog's owner, were short and to the point, and made me proud. "Touch my son," Dad said, "and you'll be lying stone cold on the floor."

Dad, a salesman, knew when to be diplomatic. This was not such a time.

Aside from a year-long duel with Heinie, life for Jerry Range in the early to mid-'50s was, as the late, famed basketball coach Al Maguire used to say, "all bubblegum and balloons."

Eleven years after I had left the lake-port city, a co-worker at the Cleveland "Plain Dealer" would refer to my shining city on the hill above the bay as "dreary Erie." He added the time-tattered cliché, "I spent a week in Erie one night."

Maybe he did, but his Erie was not my Erie. My Erie was a place of spectacular snowfalls that delighted the young Jerry Range. It was a city that had sparkling beaches on Presque Isle State Park.

It was a city of 150,000 people during a period of time when a mother could, without fear, allow her son at age 10 to take the bus to downtown to buy a Christmas present for his fourth-grade heart-throb, Betsy Bush.

It was also a city close to mountainous northwestern Pennsylvania, the forested home country of my father. The trips to his boyhood home were always special. The names had a touch of enchantment to them.

There was Titusville, where Dad always stopped at the Isaly's store to get us huge cones of rainbow ice cream (vanilla packed with walnuts, raisins and cherries); there was Oil City, site of the first discovery of oil in North America. Its riverside refineries with their Rube Goldberg-esque tangles of pipes and stacks left me awe-struck. Further up the Allegheny River was Tionesta, county seat of Forest County.

His boys would always plead with him to stop at the courthouse and show off the plaque embedded in a giant rock. The plaque attested to the fact that a Range had founded the town. Dad took great pride in reading our ancestor's exploits in the Revolutionary War.

Then a bit further up the river were East Hickory and the old family farm, about a quarter of a mile up the road from the wide and muddy Allegheny.

The nights spent at the farm were best, because the sounds were so different from those of 301 Gridley Avenue in Erie. The silence was broken by sounds of strange birds, and of stranger animals. If we were lucky, the night might be interrupted by the sight, in the faint moonlight, of a family of deer come to feed among the nearby cornstalks.

There was always a pilgrimage to the far side of the mountain to visit lonely, kindly Uncle Dink, who used his wood-fired stove to serve the best and biggest breakfasts I have ever eaten. Eggs, bacon, slabs of ham, sausage, homemade biscuits and sweet, thick jams kept appearing on the table. He was a widower and was always glad for company, always kind and generous to his city-born grand-nephews.

The downsides were the outhouses. There is no smell so bad as that of time-hardened human excrement. I learned fast to be quick in those places.

Along roads in the mountains were sparkling streams. Dad would stop the car, and we would walk to the streams. There we would see silvery mountain trout.

So in the world of Jerry Range there was both exciting city life, and adventures in the mountains only sixty miles away.

— — — — — — — — — —

Best of all in my truncated childhood was a love affair with baseball.

Many fine writers have written of the beauty and timeless grace of this sublime combination of raw sport and refined art. I can add little to what has been defined by so much talent.

I can only tell what it meant to one boy in one provincial city in one sliver of the world's time.

The game—the Little League variety—was a joyous communion of earth, sky, and I.

Whether playing in the outfield, a vast expanse of grass so green that I wanted to roll in it like a puppy, or in the infield, where I felt much more a part of the game, I knew joy. There I heard the sounds of happiness, and I was at peace with myself, with other people, and at peace with God.

It was then that I learned what Heaven is not.

Heaven is not a place of eternal quiet, broken only by the daily alleluias of the Celestial Choir. No, Heaven is a busy, bustling place filled with the joyful shouts of those who are doing what they best enjoyed doing while on Earth. In heaven, you will hear: "Hey, batta, batta, SWING, batta, batta!"

I did not know in the summer of 1955 that I was spending time in Heaven, but had someone explained it to me in those terms, it would have made sense. I would have been impatient for the game to begin, to feel the grass beneath my feet, to see a white parabola stitched against the sky as the ball rocketed toward the fielders.

I was not a particularly good baseball player—good field, no hit. I rarely embarrassed myself, though, except when the girl with black hair, green eyes and blue shorts was watching.

Then with a strange twinge in the gut, and an odd lump in the throat, my normally ball-hawking glove turned to Jell-O.

Before one game, Joe Shugart, the aggressive young coach of my Elks Club team, had me positioned at second base for pregame infield practice.

She was watching, and I knew it. The coach hit an easy hopper at me; it skittered beneath my glove and between my legs. Not one to suffer fools lightly, he banged another one at me; again it fled untouched beneath me.

Finally, he yelled, "Watch the ball, not the girl, dumb ass!"

This time, the angry grounder rocketed at me. I slid in front of it, knees flexed, glove down. I thought I had it, but there she was, and there fled the ball beneath my glove a third time.

The coach slammed the bat to the ground and headed to the dugout cursing a blue streak. I headed in and was rewarded with a smile from the girl in the blue shorts.

She had just sort of dropped into my life that final summer of childhood like a lazy fly ball floating into my glove. I didn't know how or when, but she was just there. As the ice-cream-cone summer wore on, I would come to expect her at the ball field.

When I was not playing, we would sit together in the bleachers, not talking much at all, just holding hands and enjoying the painful sweetness of being close.

After games, we would ride out to the main street, and stand astride our bikes. Then she would head west; I would watch her going down the tree-canopied street. She would turn and wave, and after a return wave I would watch until she faded from my view. Then I would head east to my neighborhood.

I never knew her name. She would remain a tiny icon in my

memory, a symbol of a childhood soon to be severed from me with meat-cleaver suddenness.

My final day on the field was an ignominious end to an undistinguished career.

My team was in the city playoffs. In fact, it would go on to plough through the playoffs and grab the city championship, winning a three-game series 2-1 against the east side champions, without me. They say that nearly 4,000 people watched each of those games.

In my first and only playoff game, I struck out three times, victim of something I had never seen before. As I dug in at the plate in my customary ninth spot in the batting order, the pitcher, a rotund 12-year-old from my school threw a pitch right at me. Bright lad that I was, I did the sensible thing: I fell flat on my backside.

"Steerike!", the umpire yelled. From my prone position, I looked at him in utter disbelief as if I were looking at a two-headed man.

"They call it a curve, kid," he said. Two more curves, two more crash landings, and an unnecessarily loud, "Steeerike three!"

I would bat twice more, and strike out twice more, although I did manage a few feeble, futile swings.

Less than a week later, the voracious microbes, now massed in an army of millions, launched their blitzkrieg attack.

Two weeks later, an overly-generous reporter for the "Erie Daily Times" in describing the Elks Club's city championship series, would write, "The Elks Club achieved victory despite being without the services of star second baseman Jerry Range, who is hospitalized with an attack of polio."

I never was a star. My childhood, so bright and glittering a few days before was gone. I would be separated from my family for far too long, with searing pain both throughout my body and in my soul.

End of Chapter One

CHAPTER 2

"2,098 Dots"

As I said before, hospitals in the 1950s made no pretext of being user-friendly.

Zem Zem, a Shriners children's hospital in Erie, was the Stalag 17 of hospitals. Apparently, its purpose was to make newly crippled children as miserable as possible. After all, many still thought it was a child's fault for becoming crippled.

Even as late as 1955, there was a lingering suspicion probably left over from the dominance of Calvinist thought that people got sick because somehow they had incurred God's displeasure.

A woman who knew my mother's aunt ran the place. That is probably why I was given one of the four door-less cubicles along the hallway leading to the ward where about 40 other children were kept. The cubicle had French-type doors allowing the room much light.

The cubicle also had 2,098 dots in the ceiling tiles. Day after boring day, I lay on my back staring at the ceiling counting the dots in one tile and then multiplying those dots by the number of ceiling tiles. It would not surprise me if there were still 2,098 dots in that cubicle's ceiling 48 years later.

Zem Zem had four things going for it: the view of the outdoors from my cubicle; a kindly old janitor who doubled as an orderly; the young, pretty therapist who treated me (she lived on my paper route), and the small, warm-water pool where twice a week I was held by that soft, sweet-smelling young woman in a swimsuit.

The best thing about the pool was entering it. The therapist would be standing chest deep in the water, a fact that caused the top of her swimsuit to balloon outward. As the elderly janitor handed me to her, the view of much of her white breasts was, well, it made my young head swim. How I looked forward to those twice-a-week pool sessions.

What I did not know, of course, was that while polio may have rendered my limbs inoperative, it had no effect on my own hormonal motor, just as it did not affect my sense of touch. Lying immobilized on my back in the fall, winter, and spring of 1955-'56, many of my muscles were atrophying. Meanwhile, one significant organ was springing to life. I rather enjoyed the sudden distensions, which happened seemingly willy-nilly.

Whatever was happening down below the belly was incomprehensible; nor did I have a usable hand for exploring. But it was quite nice. I was taking a closer look at many of the nurses and aides, and, above all, the lovely, wet and warm therapist.

What I most hungered for, though, was that bittersweet hour each Sunday when parents could visit their children. "Visit" is not quite exact. Parents could talk to their child, but they were warned never to touch the love-starved child. A rope was strung the length of the hallway past the cubicle entrances and down through the wards past the end of each bed.

Woe to the parent who stepped under that rope to hug or kiss a child! If the martinette who ran the place, or one of her lieutenants, spotted such an unthinkable transgression, the parent would be asked to leave.

Soon after my move to Zem Zem from a hospital in Erie for contagious diseases (polio and tuberculosis), my family left Erie to join my father in Dover, Ohio, 170 miles distant from Erie. Dad had gotten his long-hoped-for promotion from salesman with a propane gas company to manager of a small outlet in Dover.

It was at the end of his first day on the new job that my mother had to call him and say between sobs, "Jerry's in the hospital with polio." Brimming with things to tell his devoted young wife about the new job, his bubble was savagely burst and his pride at his new accomplishment—one that he had waited 10 years for—lay on the floor in the jagged pieces of two broken hearts 170 miles apart.

The evil microbes did a devilish jig that night.

Every week after the family had left Erie, they would make the Sunday trek for the one-hour visit. This of course was before the advent of interstate highways. How they must have suffered. The stress, tension, and worry must have strained my parent's relationship to the limit. Yes, they loved each other. But the daily concern over a young son 170 miles distant, the unfulfilling weekly trip for a one-hour visit and the difficulties in adapting to a new community must have been almost too much heavy baggage for a marriage.

Somehow, my parents managed to hang onto their marriage despite the intensity of the trauma they were battling. Their staying together is, to me, a powerful statement of the unbreakable bond between them.

Only after my own children were born was I able to put into some context what my parents went through.

Above all else, parents fear seeing their children suffer. Possibly the worst week of my life came when Jerry Jr., then about age 7, developed either spinal meningitis or polio. I literally trembled when I thought of the possible nightmares awaiting him. Fortunately, he was not permanently physically affected.

Severely crippled people develop tunnel vision, which allows them to focus on their own survival and their rehabilitation training, which most often centers on developing "life skills."

That is a phrase in the rehab trade which simply means developing the ability to do things which many people never even think about—feeding oneself, washing oneself, brushing one's teeth, wiping one's butt, and putting on clothes without the help of others.

These energy-sapping maneuvers put blinders on crippled people to the sufferings of others, especially the sufferings of able-bodied people.

Severely crippled people also develop a martyr complex. Small wonder when other people are telling them constantly how much they suffer, poor things. Many handicapped people are, indeed, able to handle gracefully daily discomfort, frustration, and even torment.

However, they are jealous of their turf: they do not want to share the emotional limelight with others, with another cripple or with an able-bodied family member who gets ill.

For instance, I have plenty of daily aches, pains, and frustrations, which by now are like old friends. I can co-exist with them, often fitfully, but I long ago reached an accord with my aches, pains, and for the past 14 years, incredible itching in the pubic area. I am no longer able to change positions while sitting in the wheelchair. This causes a continuous fungal itch of almost mythic intensity that far surpasses mere annoyance.

It is very annoying when a member of my family takes ill.

How dare they! I am the one who is supposed to get attention because of a bodily difficulty.

Before I got back to the family, there was a medical emergency of which I had no knowledge at the time. Dad developed a bleeding ulcer in 1955-'56 that nearly put him under the surgeon's knife. He was a three-pack-a-day Winston smoker. Just four days before he was scheduled for surgery, he called a doctor in Akron who had been recommended by one of Dad's acquaintances in his company.

The doctor told him, "If you quit smoking cold turkey, and stick to this diet that I'm going to give you, then I think we can avoid surgery." Back then, there was no medical literature yet that linked ulcers with bacteria, and of course there were no ulcer medications such as Zantac, or others that were given by prescription only and now are sold over the counter.

My younger brother, Jim, then 4, would get car sick during each Sunday trip, no doubt a result of the bad vibrations emanating from his parents.

It is not hard to imagine the Sundays on which my mother, my father, and Jim would prepare for the round-trip of nearly six hours. (Older brother Tom would stay with the family's new acquaintances). Although Erie is only 170 miles from Dover, Ohio, there were no interstate highways. For the most part, until one reached Route 20 along the Lake Erie shore, there were only two-lane roads that meandered from the downtown of one small town or to another.

For instance, a trip from Dover to Erie would take travelers through (this list is by no means comprehensive) the Ohio communities of Mineral City; Magnolia; Waynesville; Malvern; Minerva; Alliance; Salem; Newton Falls; Canfield; a detour around the large city of Youngstown, Girard, Andover, Ashtabula, Conneaut, Ohio; then Springfield, Pa., Fairview; Girard; Millcreek Twp., and finally Zem Zem on Erie's west side.

To make the 1 p.m. deadline, the family would have to leave Dover no later than 5 a.m. in case of traffic delays. The tension was stomach-churning and brain-tightening. It probably evidenced itself in cutting remarks between my parents and in too-sharp commands to my little brother, 4 years of age.

"Goddamit, Mary, where are my good shoes?" he shouted from his closet in the TV room on one such Sunday morning.

"They are right where you put them last night after you polished them," she snapped right back.

"If you would keep things in the same place, you might not always be running around like a chicken with its head cut off yelling that the sky is falling," she added.

That was greeted by more curses. They were good people, but they were under the strain of that weekly crushing burden and the never-ending heaviness of heart over their sick child far away. In those days, there were no such things as "support groups." If people had to suffer and to struggle, they usually did it alone.

Early on at Zem Zem, I had complained of the food to my parents. One meal sticks in my memory like hardened, day-old egg yolk to a dirty plate. Without fail every Tuesday night, we were served poached eggs and cold beets, first-class culinary sadism.

How many children do you know plead for beets and poached eggs?

My parents thumbed their noses at the no-go-under-the-rope-and-love-your-child prohibition. Dad would stand guard while

Mom slipped under the cockamamie Maginot Line. First, there would come a hug and a kiss, then a few hurried bites of her fried chicken. She would then retreat, and stand guard for Dad.

This nonsensical tag-team ballet made necessary by the cruel rope rule would go on for an hour. Far too quickly, the hour would have fled, and the tears would come, flooding my face and dampening the top of my hospital gown.

Thank God I was still young enough to cry! I had that purgative ability well into my twenties until I was a junior in college. My inability to cry later on as an adult would contribute to a deepening depressed state.

The memory of the annoying rope rule is nothing compared to the memory of the young girl, a burn victim, about my age in the nearest cubicle. We called out to each other, not really having a conversation, but offering the other the knowledge that there was someone our age who cared. I dreaded the nights when it came time for the changing of her dressings. Her screams echo in a tiny spot in my brain in a night that never sees the dawn.

"Mama, Mama, help me, Mama! It hurts so bad, it hurts so bad! Mama, help me, oooh, oooh, please stop, please stop!"

I desperately wanted to cover my ears with my hands, but of course I could not lift them off the bed. So I had to listen to the poor girl's agony.

On the few occasions that we saw each other, I learned what torment looked like—a pale, grayish face that wanted to smile but had no place for a smile with sunken, dark brown eyes circled by wrinkles. The 12-year-old had the face of an old woman.

In the cubicle beyond that occupied by the burned girl was a teenager who had been made into a quadriplegic in a traffic accident. He had great trouble moving his bowels. About every four nights, that difficulty would require the night nurse to give him an enema. The sounds of pumping water, his groaning, the nurse's obvious disgust, and the smell—oh, my God, the smell!—are with me 48 years later.

During my year at Zem Zem, I would lie on my back (counting tile spots and multiplying) wiggling the fingers of my right hand where there was some "return," the term used for regained muscle strength. I tried over a long period—lasting seven months—after leaving the infectious stage of polio in the first month to "crawl" my hand up over my hip bone onto my abdomen.

One day, it simply happened. Up came the thumb, the index finger, the middle finger, and the final two. Next, I worked on moving the hand up the belly, up the chest to the face, and back down again. Over and over, hour after hour, day after day, I kept up the hand's round trip. At the same time, strength was returning in my back and stomach muscles, allowing me to sit in the cranked-up hospital bed longer and longer.

One evening, as I was sitting up in bed, an attendant brought my evening meal. Minutes went by and no one came to feed me, which did not bother me because I did not like having someone feed me anyway even if it meant going without an occasional meal. I "crawled" my hand to the fork, forced it into a poorly-baked potato, leaned over, and somehow put the fork into my mouth.

My shout of victory brought people running into my cubicle. I repeated the process for them, and got a round of applause.

The other time when people gathered in my cubicle was when "Days of Our Lives" came on TV in mid-afternoon. My mother's Aunt Dot, who was the Secretary for a small Catholic insurance company, had bought me a new TV—no small thing in 1955. Soon after the gift arrived, nurses began hanging around my cubicle in the afternoon hours to watch soap operas. They could not catch a line drive, nor did they know where second base was, but at least they were human company for a very lonely boy.

Of all of us crowded into the cubicle to watch "Days of Our Lives," I was probably the only one who really understood the opening line of that daily soap: "Like sand through the hour glass, so are the days of our lives." That described my life perfectly.

One warm early October day, my Little League team showed up outside my cubicle. A nurse opened the doors briefly, and my coach gave me a ball used in the championship game. There were brave words all around; then a sort of embarrassed silence broken only by the shuffling of feet. The nurse gently shooed the team away, saying that I must not risk catching cold.

I never saw any of my teammates again. Only a few names stay with me—star pitcher Russ Etter, who had at least 10 no-hitters to his credit; diminutive catcher "Pinky" Higgins; first baseman/pitcher Russ May; shortstop Jimmy Dwyer; outfielder/pitcher Donnie Basto; a boy named Miller, who could hit anything thrown near the plate, and a lad named Sheen, whom young coach Joe Shugart called "Bishop." There were more, but the years have stolen their names from me and have caused their images to fade beyond recall.

I loved them all.

A near-sighted aide earned my hate. She wore thick glasses, the kind folks used to compare to the thick bottoms of Coca-Cola bottles. She was the designated finger-nail cutter. Yes, the nurses' aide who practically had to feel her way down the hall was given the chore of cutting children's nails. She ignored my impassioned entreaties to be careful and belittled me as she cut away with a pair of small manicuring scissors.

How I dreaded her weekly round! I gritted my teeth, closed my eyes, and tried not to cry out in pain at the nipping of skin.

Lying in my cubicle, I would fantasize about having spigots connected to hoses that upon my voice command—in the pre-computer age my 11-year-old mind assumed some sort of machinery developed by the military would power the complicated system. In those early days of the Cold War, there was always talk on the radio, TV, and in movie newsreels of the limitless ability of our military minds to stay one step ahead of the Red Menace.

It was not important in my fantasies who had developed a system that could give me on voice command chocolate milk, Hire's Root Beer, and Coca-Cola (real Americans drank Coca-Cola; drinkers of wimpy Pepsi were suspect).

The system was only in my mind of course, but my desire for the drinks that had always pleased me were real and unattainable. If there were a soft drink machine in the hospital, its contents certainly would have been out of bounds for patients. Thirst was a constant companion, particularly at night.

My mother had found a cup that had a rounded top to it. In the top was a hole through which a plastic straw was inserted and when the straw was inserted, there was little leakage of water. One night, my thirst seemed unbearable. Time after time, I called, "Nurse, nurse, please give me some water."

Maybe it was five minutes or five hours. I had no sense of the passage of time. She finally appeared in the doorway of the cubicle and severely tongue-lashed me.

"You are not the only patient in this hospital," she hissed. "Shame on you for being such a baby." But she did put some water into the contraption that my mother had brought and laid it on the bed at a 90-degree angle to my mouth in such a way that she could hurry away, and I could sip the five or six ounces of precious liquid.

Her contempt for me remains as clear as one of the mountain streams that we used to see near my father's old homestead. Her words stung, but I got some short relief from the thirst.

The treatment I got from her and from the sadistic skin clipper illustrates something that I learned over and over again in many more hospitals. No matter how advanced the medical treatment, no matter how inspired the professional medical geniuses, nothing is accomplished if the bedside nursing is bad or uninspired.

Ultimately, it is the spirit and the will to live in the patient that will mean success or failure in what medical professionals like to call "protocols," or in laymen's terms, "treatment."

There were two Zem Zem "cocktails" worthy of note. Every day we were made to drink a glass of tomato juice laced with the bitter-tasting mineral, iron. To this day, I cannot drink tomato juice without gagging, due to that foul concoction at Zem Zem.

If one had the misfortune of not having had a bowel movement—one that passed muster—for a length of three days, then it was time for the mineral oil, a clear, incredibly thick, oily syrup. No normal human being could drink it without gagging. We were forced to drink it.

After nearly a year of Zem Zem's rope trick, beets, and mineral oil, I was shocked and then ecstatic at the sight of my father getting out of his car not 20 yards from my cubicle on a Friday. Then my mother walked into the cubicle from the hallway, her face a beatific glow.

"Sweetheart, we have arranged for your transfer to a hospital in Akron, near us," she said. My heart leapt, despite the presence of the supervisor. My father lifted me easily in his powerful arms. The supervisor who had hair touched with gray and pulled back in a severe bun and whose arms were folded below breasts the shape of sagging artillery shells, said, "Jerry, you can come back to us anytime you want."

"When will hell freeze over?" I thought.

On the way out of Erie, my father stopped at a drugstore. I asked why. "I'm going to buy you a urinal," he said matter-of-factly. "That means I'm going home!" I shouted. He nodded yes. Tears plentiful enough to fill nearby Lake Erie fell in a soothing flood of joy.

My parents had been directed to Dr. Walter A Hoyt Jr., of Akron, an orthopedist widely respected in northeast Ohio. When they told him that I had been separated from the family for a year, he looked at my mother and said firmly, "You get that boy home for a week, and love him." My parents explained that Dr. Hoyt wanted me to come to Akron Children's Hospital for an evaluation.

On the eve of my second leaving, I lay awake, begging God for the full use of my arms if I had to re-enter the hospital world. I sobbed and yelled, "Please, God, at least give me the use of my arms!"

God did not reveal if he had heard me, although I guessed he had, because my mother entered the room and said, "Jerry, you'll wake the dead shouting like this." She held me until I fell into a fitful sleep.

The next day I found myself in Akron Children's Hospital. (God had not granted my request; I really don't recall being surprised).

My first question of the eminent and kindly Dr. Hoyt, who looked as if he had sent by Central Casting from Hollywood, was, "When can I go home?"

My stay in Akron Children's left me only with two memories: one of watching my roommate throw up something greenish after his tonsillectomy. The second is of an understandably peeved Dr. Hoyt answering my never-ending query, "When can I go home?" with a gruff, "Tomorrow, damn it!"

He kept his word. I did go home the next day, but my stay would be disappointingly brief.

End of Chapter Two

CHAPTER 3

"Hill Country Sex Ed, Bambi, FDR"

The next destination after Akron Children's Hospital was Warm Springs, Ga., about 600 miles southwest of Dover, Ohio.

From the early 1930s until the late 1950s, polio was America's glamor disease, as AIDS was in the 1990s—the "disease du jour," if you will, of its time.

Warm Springs was the world's pre-eminent treatment center for people who had been slapped down by polio. We were called "post-polios."

People from all over the country who had children crippled by polio tried to get their children admitted to Warm Springs. Like anything else in life, it is not who you are but who you know that opens doors in the world of medicine.

Dr. Hoyt had a good friend who was a family practitioner in Dover, 45 miles south of Akron. That doctor had added our family to his practice.

The county chapter of the March of Dimes needed a new president. My father agreed to serve. Those two things sealed the deal and opened the door to Warm Springs for me.

My parents were relieved and thankful. I was not so sanguine, and did not shrink from making my feelings known. It meant another open-ended, painful separation after about only three weeks with the family.

What my father said was law in his family, and this is how he laid down the law to his crippled son:

"Jerry, we have a wonderful opportunity for you to start to get better. It means you'll have to spend some time where there are a lot of people who know a whole lot about taking care of young people like you with polio."

"But, Dad, I don't want to leave again and . . ."

He shut me off saying, "I know you don't, Jer, but it just has to be done. We will leave for Georgia in about 10 days."

Frankly, I was becoming a bit of a pain in the ass. My constant crying and my constant need for intensive nursing weighed heavily on my father, mother, and two brothers. They all looked forward to some respite. My parents were genuinely excited at the prospect of my receiving world-class treatment.

"Insight" is not in the vocabulary of most 12-year-old boys. It never occurred to me that I might be a burden to the family. All I knew was that again I would be alone among strangers and far from the family.

The Warm Springs Foundation was the crown jewel of the National Foundation for Infantile Paralysis, better known as the March of Dimes, for decades the country's favorite charity drive.

Warm Springs, a sleepy southwest-Georgia hamlet in piney-woods hill country, had two resources that put it on the map. The first was indeed a warm spring. The water always was 88 degrees. A small spa industry had grown up around the spring.

It would have remained a commercial backwater were it not for Franklin D. Roosevelt, elected four times to the presidency beginning in 1932.

After getting polio in 1921, Roosevelt was persuaded to try the waters at Warm Springs. FDR was a strong-willed man who, once convinced of the efficacy of something, put his considerable clout behind it. He fell in love with Warm Springs, its warm-hearted people, and the pine-covered hills. He poured more than half of his personal fortune into building a center for the treatment of polio patients at the springs.

Later, he would establish his little White House in the tiny town of Warm Springs.

Early in FDR's presidency, First Lady Eleanor Roosevelt became the hostess for an annual top-shelf White House charity ball that began the fund drive for the March of Dimes.

A ticket to the ball quickly became an absolute necessity for the "swells" of high society in New York City, Washington, and Hollywood.

There was no store in America from Macy's in New York City to a mom-and-pop store in Keokuk, Iowa, that did not have a March of Dimes' donation can.

The Tuscarawas County, Ohio, chapter of the March of Dimes paid my bill. The pennies, nickels, and dimes from a population base of 75,000 people covered well over $5,000, no small amount in 1957.

Off we went in mid-September.

One more time in what was now almost a ritual, I begged to be spared another hospital incarceration: "Dad," I said while turning on the water works, "I just cannot live without you and Mom."

His look said this would be the last conversation on the subject. "Jerry, if you do not get treatment here you just might not live much longer, and if you do live longer, your life will be like that of Uncle Shell's."

Uncle Shell (his given name was Shellous) had polio when he was a child. Only one leg was seriously damaged. But in the early part of the 20th century, a crippling disease meant that a person would not be considered useful. Shell became the family's "cross." He could walk with a cane, but the family treated him like a baby. The other children were told to do for him anything with the slightest degree of difficulty.

He was sent to Erie after some of his brothers went there. There, he could get handouts from private charities and collect a small amount of state aid. He and his wife, rotund and peevish, lived in a tenement. Once, my father took me to see Uncle Shell. The stairwell smelled of urine. The place was noisy, and the floors had crumpled candy and cigarette wrappers strewn about, as well as the butts of cigarettes and cigars.

Their apartment was filthy. "Get me out of here!" was my mentally-telepathic message to my dad. So in September 1956 in Warm Springs, when my dad suggested that I might end up like Uncle Shell, the words were like a splash of cold water on my face.

After a two-day trip, we found ourselves driving up a road cut through the forest past white cottages. We emerged in front of an immaculate, long, white-columned building.

It was Georgia Hall, named for the Georgia citizens who had contributed to its being built. Everything in Georgia Hall, from the long, oaken registry desk at one end to the elegant dining room at the other, spoke of understated good taste. Everything was bright and airy because of the floor-to-ceiling windows that ran the length of the 100-foot-long hall. Rich green vegetation merged with flowers with colors that ran the gamut of the rainbow just outside the windows.

This was definitely not like Zem Zem Children's Hospital in Erie.

The hospital buildings were around a huge quadrangle filled with pine, dogwood, magnolia trees, and azaleas. There were verandahs everywhere; a huge one was behind Georgia Hall, where relatives of patients met in the sweet Georgia evenings, and often formed lasting friendships. On other verandahs, patients would take the evening air.

The spirit of FDR was palpable. My favorite place was a grotto where in brick bas-relief there was FDR in his wheelchair reaching out to a young girl on crutches and wearing leg braces. On the wall was his famed quotation from his first inaugural speech: "We have nothing to fear but fear itself."

Also on the wall was a quote that still rings a bell 48 years later: "While they were saying among themselves it could not be done, it was done." Lingering all about was the optimism of FDR, the feeling you get when you see old photos of that buoyant man with cigarette in cigarette holder pushing upward at a jaunty angle in his great half-moon of a smile.

Many staff members had known FDR personally, some going back to when he presided over Thanksgiving or Christmas meals for patients and staff. The unforced optimism was infectious, and for five days a week Monday through Friday, a patient had little time to brood.

This was the only hospital of which I could ever truly say that the futures of the patients were of uppermost importance. I have been a patient in 12 of them. Hospitals in TV commercials say that patients are not profit-producing commodities, or that the opinions of patients matter. I do not believe it.

At Warm Springs the patient's opinions on treatment were given great weight. The patient was a human being first, second, and third.

After returning from a short Florida vacation, my parents stopped briefly before heading back to Ohio. "How can they do this to me," I asked God, the nurses, my roommates—anyone who would listen.

They were leaving an emotionally distraught descendant of a Union defender at the battle of Gettysburg to the mercy of a bunch of yahoos who spoke like slow-on-the-uptake Canadians. They were never able to utter a sentence without saying "y'all," much as the crazy Canucks cannot speak a sentence without ending it with an "eh?"

When my parents left, I sobbed again. I would not see them until Christmas. This time, however, I was not left to poached eggs, beets, and inconsistent treatment.

This time, there were caring nurses, all of them attractive enough in their tight, starched white uniforms to keep my curious new organ between my legs at nearly constant attention. Even their way of speaking was strangely erotic: those soft, beckoning Georgia drawls that dripped sweetness over you.

The food was excellent. Moving at its own slowed-down pace, the Foundation nevertheless moved with a purpose that would not allow a patient time to dwell upon the wounds suffered from the slings and arrows of fate's caprice.

As my sobbing sputtered out, I realized that three other youngsters were studying me.

My roommates were what now would be called an experiment in "cultural diversity." There was the horny Richie from Boston, a moderately-crippled teenager who could sing a new song called "Don't Be Cruel" by someone with the obviously fake name of "Elvis Presley."

Richie spent his evenings putting his uncrippled arms to use while necking with a cute girl in a wheelchair. They cared not a whit about my watching. She was Mary Lou Breslin, who hailed from Louisville, Ky. The second roommate was a south-Georgia boy named Billy, whose peanut-growing father often brought a bagful of unripened peanuts. Billy and his father instructed me in the art of sucking the goobers.

The third roommate was J.D. Cobb, from some distant holler in the misty Smokey Mountains of eastern Tennessee. J.D. was older than I—by at least two years, and more knowledgeable in a subject I was becoming keenly interested in—sex.

J.D. Cobb talked to me of something mysterious—the vagina, or as he called it, the "sugar hill." He spoke of strange tents at carnivals that yearly visited the mysterious uplands from where he came.

"Jeery," he said in a conspiratorial whisper, leaning toward me in his bed, "mah brother said he went in one of them big ol' tents and danged if a girl with no clothes on sure 'nough rubbed a Co-Cola bottle rat there 'tween 'er legs. Mah brother says it cost him two whole dollars to get in that thar tent."

Then he astounded me when he said that I could shoot some white stuff from my new active organ into a woman and make a baby.

"Honest?" I asked.

"Yup," he said.

That news shook my world like a 9.0 Richter scale earthquake would clobber California.

While I was trying to process this apocalyptic data, the prettiest nurse on our floor, a full-busted young woman with shoulder-length chest-nut-colored hair and emerald eyes, came in, leaned up against the bottom of my bed with her hand resting on a perfectly-rounded hip and asked, "Is there any thang I can do for y'all?"

After she had left and when I had caught my breath, I turned to J.D. Cobb and asked incredulously, "You mean I could make a baby in her?"

"Yup," he said.

"Do you think she'd do it for me?" I asked, panting.

"Nope," the Tennessee sage said.

Aside from the rough-hewn lessons on the mechanics of sex given freely by J.D. Cobb, there were other lessons that Warm Springs taught.

It taught me that I was severely crippled, and that I was destined to remain severely crippled the rest of my life.

That sounds odd, considering the previous 13 months—the three weeks of high fever and pain, the long months of total immobility, the generalized paralysis, and the shuttling in and out of hospitals.

I had entered the world of crippling as a child. Children have little sense of time or the future, and an even looser grasp on reality—a factor that is often a defense mechanism. Also, I had seen very few other crippled children in those 13 months, being cloistered in my cubicle at Zem Zem.

At Warm Springs, puberty was behind me, or at least I was beyond the crest of the wave. Second, a sense of a future was forming. Third, there were crippled youths everywhere, and their omnipresence was a mirror. In that mirror, I saw myself—a severely crippled youth, one who would be crippled the rest of his life.

There would be no lightning bolt from on high that would make me able-bodied again.

My sense now of that place in 1956-'57 was an attitude that said: "Of course you are physically limited. We can't change that, so let's get on with finding your route to success."

When "Bambi" Cranmore walked into my life, I had another diversion from my homesickness. Charlotte "Bambi" Cranmore, late of the University of North Carolina, was short, slim and shapely in her well-filled-out white uniform with the blue patch of a graduate physical therapist over her tight right breast that with its twin pushed hard against her uniform. Her short, light-brown hair framed a lightly-freckled face with eyes of sweet Carolina blue.

Bambi's bouncy walk, her bubbly voice with its "y'alls," "you sweet thang," and "Mornin', Shugah," and her constant smile lit up a room. In those days, she was what people called "perky."

She was my designated "PT," or physical therapist.

Directing Bambi and the other PT's was Ann Martin, a sturdy, square-cut woman with short brown hair, glasses, and a ruddy complexion. She was in her early 40s. It certainly looked like she meant business as she stood astride the hallway on my first day at physical therapy.

"In here please," she said to the black "push boy," pointing to her open office door.

She was a formidable chunk of humanity. I was scared to death.

"Do you know why you are here?" she asked.

"I, I, uh . . ." was my response.

"You are here to learn how to take care of yourself so that you can be a positive force in the world; to become independent of your parents and other family members; to be truly your own person and not just another handicapped person dependent upon charity or the government," she said. "We will give you the tools to do those things. Then you must build your future," she said, adding, "now get to work."

Warm Springs looked more like a college campus than a collection of hospital units. First East and Second East—the main living areas for most patients, Surgical, and Georgia Hall, as well as administrative units stood around the long quadrangle.

All the buildings were white-washed. The corset shop and the world-famed brace shop were both free-standing beyond the quadrangle.

About half a dozen women worked in the corset shop. Corsets were critical, because teenagers grew quickly and our spines had to be supported properly or scoliosis, curvature of the spine, would threaten slow suffocation as the curving spine eventually could collapse the lungs. My corset and I were inseparable companions for five years.

The brace shop was the place where miracles in metal and leather were commonplace. Long leg braces could be made and corrected as the attending doctor ordered, in a day's time.

Surgeons in the 1950s at Warm Springs routinely transplanted tendons taken from a leg into the palm side of a thumb to give a patient an opposable thumb again. Also treated with bone grafts were many people with severe scoliosis. The bone grafts worked like interior braces forcing the spine to grow straight.

The only time I saw surgical patients was at the theater, where twice a week we saw first-run flicks.

Those gutsy kids, most of them in full-length body casts, were a hardy lot. Many would be lying on their sides on their gurneys with a rubber line trailing from their midsections to a large bottle on the shelf below. Periodically, a cascade of urine would splash into one of the bottles. After a few times, one would stop looking. Once you have seen one pot of pee, you have seen them all.

When a patient first entered Warm Springs, he or she underwent a thorough, stem-to-stern evaluation. Then the patient was assigned to a team of nurses, occupational therapists (OTs), physical therapists (PTs), and the psychologist. Heading the team would be a senior staff orthopedist in consultation with an internist, and several young orthopedists.

The gathering of this group took place with the patient present. The thoughts of the patient, no matter the age, were given great weight. The gatherings were called "Clinic," and a patient's style of life for weeks to come was decided in "Clinic."

The presiding orthopedist sought information from all present. It was tense, because careers often rose or fell on what happened in "Clinic."

The most important and most desired of all breakthroughs for a patient was decided in "Clinic." What all patients sought and what was held out as the visible proof of their progress was permission to take the noon-day and evening meals in Georgia Hall's elegant dining room.

The black maitre'd in impeccable black suit with a white shirt and black tie ran the dining hall with an iron fist.

The reward was worth a patient's blood, sweat, and tears. The cuisine—not "food"—was superb. Black waiters in white jackets, black trousers, white shirts, and black ties served meals. The dining area itself had wall-to-ceiling windows; the carpeting and other accouterments such as crystal goblets were first-class.

Patients were seated first. There was no deviation. It did not matter if the governor of Georgia were present; he had to wait until the maitre 'd said he could enter. Next to be seated after the patients were staff members. Then visitors and tourists were seated.

After the evening meal, patients were allowed to stay in Georgia Hall's recreation rooms, or sit outside on the verandah and watch the night pull its blanket tenderly over southwestern Georgia. A patient might visit the candy shop, where newspapers and magazines were on sale.

It was there that the insidious germ, "journalismus careeritis," first attacked. The Atlanta papers were especially attractive. The slogan of the "Constitution" was forthright: "The South's Standard Newspaper for over a Hundred Years." However, the slogan of the "Journal" was the clear winner: "Covers Dixie Like the Dew." Was there ever a catchier newspaper slogan?

The manner in which a patient got to daily appointments was a remnant of the old South. The patient was wheeled to and fro by "push boys," all of them African-Americans in today's politically correct world; "neegrahs" in west Georgia of the mid-'50s.

The black push boys and the black orderlies fascinated me. In my 11-year childhood in Erie, Pa., I had very little contact with blacks, although there was at the time, I am told, a sizable black community. There were no blacks at Jefferson Elementary, a school of nearly a thousand pupils.

The only black I can recall seeing on anything approaching a regular basis was a wizened man of indeterminate age who passed a hat at semi-pro baseball games played at the city-run park near our neighborhood. White adults called him "Moon." No first name; no last name, just Moon.

As he walked along the front rows of the bleachers, he had a standard sing-song to prompt people to pitch money into his hat. "I thank ya, and I thank ya; I thank ya, and I thank ya; I thank ya, and I thank ya," he would call out, over and over.

Scouring my memory brings no recollection of another black in Erie, a city then of 150,000 people. What makes that so astonishing is that after I reached 10, my parents let me ride the bus alone to downtown, and browse in the department stores. Surely there must have been blacks on the streets and in the stores, yet I cannot recall seeing even one.

Blacks were vilified in my environment. They were "untermensch," somehow not fully human. They were not good "things" to be near. So when I saw blacks other than Moon, I believe that my mind unconsciously erased them from my memory. I was being true to my environment, a Caucasian sea.

Among cripples, there was a pecking order. In 1962 most cripples were "untermensch" to most able-bodied people. At the top in our sub-class were post-polios who had strong arms. In the No. 2 slot were post-polios who had some involvement in all four limbs. At No. 3 were paraplegics, people whose spines had been broken in the lower back. Next came quadriplegics, people with spines severed in the neck.

Last on the hit parade were people with cerebral palsy, a congenital motor disorder that evidenced itself in many ways— from simple difficulty, say, in using one hand to the inability to speak. There always is someone you can look down upon.

At Warm Springs, blacks made up a large part of the manual-labor workforce. I was certainly aware that they were second-class members of the Warm Springs "family." For instance, they could not eat in the Georgia Hall dining room. Such things bothered me a great deal, especially after I got to know several blacks.

There was an orderly named Sam, who every morning would open the door to our room and say in a sarcastic caricature voice, "Who's in dis heah house sayin,' 'Who's in dis heah house'?"

Beyond the caricature greeting was a fine and funny human being. There was another orderly called "Big Seese."

Cecil was his name. He was tall, lanky, and very caring. He would gently lift me and carry me to a small bathroom with a commode safely placed between two short walls with metal railings. Every few minutes, Cecil would check on me.

Cecil was as gentle and kind a hospital worker as any other person who served me in eleven other hospitals. He was a true gentleman of the South, old or new.

On the other hand, there was a white orderly named Billy Joe, who daily regaled me with detailed stories of his sexual exploits from the night before.

"You should have seen it! I banged her till she hollered for mercy at least a hundred times. There were spots all over the bed last night, kid!"

So Warm Springs taught me to judge people by the contents of their hearts. That alone would have been reason enough to go to Warm Springs.

As indicated earlier, the brace shop was the crowning jewel. It is not stretching the truth to call the craftsmen who worked in that shining-white little shop "artisans."

What they did with metal and leather was miraculous. Due to their efforts, thousands left Warm Springs outfitted with braces, feeding systems, hand splints, and other orthopedic devices that not only helped a person function in the outside world, but were comfortable.

The men running the brace shop would not accept a lukewarm "yes" when they asked a patient if an orthopedic device felt good. If the answer were not a ringing affirmative, back the device would go to the workbench until the patient, and his or her doctor, was satisfied.

The brace shop worked in close harmony with the arcane little corset shop. There, those sweet ladies—and I consciously and deliberately use that term—stitched and sewed the day long, making corsets exactly to doctors' orders. Those corsets were sent to the brace shop for the precisely placed and enormously critical metal phalanges at the top and bottom of the back of the corset. They were set at precise angles to force the spine over time to grow straight.

Two Northerners who had adapted to the Warm Springs' way of doing business deserve special mention, for each was instrumental in my finding a path to the future.

Grace Marie Fryman, who headed the Foundation's psychology unit, quickly sized up my potential, and never stopped encouraging me to reach for a star. My regret is that I did not name one of my two daughters after the gentle Iowa woman of soft words and firm ideas.

As described, Ann Martin was a solid chunk of Wisconsin womanhood who ran the staff of physical therapists with a firm hand. In many talks with me, she mixed just the right amount of goad with just the right amount of goodness and understanding.

Both Miss Fryman and Miss Martin were Catholics, and saw to it that I received the sacraments of Confession, which I was beginning to need on a regular basis, and Communion each week.

It was Miss Martin who assigned Bambi Cranmore to my case, which included the wonderful, unintentionally sensual "Plus One."

"Plus One" was a system devised to allow one able-bodied person to move a severely crippled person from bed to wheelchair, or from wheelchair to a seat including the toilet without using mechanical aids.

Basically, the able-bodied person placed his or her hands under the buttocks of the crippled person while locking the person's weak knees against the mover's. Then the two would rock back and forth until the crippled person was standing with his chin hooked over the shoulder of the mover. The mover would shuffle the other's feet until a transfer had been accomplished.

The method never impressed me, but I greatly appreciated the law of unintended consequences. It meant, in effect, that I would be for several minutes in exquisite embrace with a Dixie delight, my beautiful therapist, Bambi Cranmore.

What a wonderful co-mingling of function and fun.

Five months went by in which I got the best rehabilitation training available in the world. Add precise brace and corset fittings, and my getting the brass ring of dining in Georgia Hall. Then in Clinic, my orthopedist stunned me: "Jerry, it's time for you to go home and start your new life."

The pleasures of "Plus One" and Bambi Cranmore paled next to those words.

It was time to be homeward-bound, even if that home was in a new state and town. After 18 months of near-total separation from my family, the site of reunion meant little.

Home to Mom. Home to Dad. Home to Tom. Home to Jim.

My long heartache, as I neared 13, with my truncated childhood now a fading memory, was over.

"Operator, I'd like to place a collect call to the Range residence in Dover, Ohio."

"Hello, Range residence."

"Dad, they say I can come home—to stay."

"We'll be there in two days, son."

"Hurry, Dad."

The phone was taken from my trembling right hand and placed on its cradle by a nurse with tears streaming down her face, too.

End of Chapter Three

CHAPTER 4

"A Wheelchair in Dover, The Coach, The Girl"

Father Pius Kaelin had been a theology professor at Catholic University in Washington, D.C. As a resident of the St. Joseph rectory, he would visit "shut-ins."

His newest "shut-in" was also Dover's newest full-time cripple—me. Every Saturday morning, Mom would prepare a small altar with a crucifix, holy oil, a white cloth, and holy water. Father Pius would say some prayers in Latin.

Then he would intone the words intended by the Catholic Church for the anointing of the sick: "Sprinkle me, O Lord, with hyssop, wash me and I shall be whiter than snow. My help is in the name of the Lord, who made heaven and earth."

All the while, he would be dousing me with holy water. No one ever got hyssoped more than I did.

Father Pius was a stickler for regular weekly confessions. How many sins can a 14-year-old commit while bracketed in corset and long leg braces and sitting in a wheelchair? It was a struggle to come up with enough sins to make the confession worth his while:

"Bless me, Father, for I have sinned. It has been a week since my last confession. In that time, I said 'damn' six times; I looked down a girl's blouse when she bent over to pick up the pencil that I dropped in school (that trick always brought a view of young, white breast). And I called my brother a dirty name twice."

The Catholic Church, like the rest of American society in the 1950s, regarded handicapped people as being "sick."

In Christ's time, lameness, blindness, or other physical disfigurements were symbols of sin; somehow a person's being crippled was seen as punishment by God.

In the Gospels, Christ cured many as a metaphor to show His power over sin. The nagging notion—that somehow being crippled was a punishment by God—still lingered nearly 2,000 years later. Physical suffering, the church now teaches, is God's way of drawing someone closer to him. God is a compassionate being, not a sadist.

The small city of Dover, Ohio, population about 11,000, and the Catholic community within it, did not know what to do with me in 1957. Society had not yet given handicapped individuals first-class citizenship. Many regarded a person in a wheelchair with distaste, loathing, and fear—"There but for the grace of God go I."

Conversely, others looked upon me as being some sort of person upon whom God had bestowed a certain kind of extra-human quality—sort of a human good luck charm.

From the very first days of my return to the family, I was called upon to make other people feel good by accepting what they believed would make me feel happy. We lived 80 miles from Cleveland, where my maternal grandparents were at the time. The rift between my father and mother and her parents never really closed, but necessity drove my mother's parents to seek my father's financial help.

My grandfather was a simple man; a hard-working mechanic whose wife made fast and loose with every dollar he made.

My grandfather said he knew an usher at old Cleveland Municipal Stadium. He told us his friend could get us good seats. Despite my father's obvious displeasure, we drove to Cleveland in the summer of 1957 and met my grandparents at the stadium.

On the way into the stadium, the officious usher made a great show of opening a gate, yelling loudly: "Make way for the cripple! Make way for the cripple!"

In the world of "cripples," "handicapped people," or "physically challenged," it is the same as in the world of an Italian-American or in the world of African-Americans. Italians can call other Italians "dagos," and African-Americans can call other African-Americans "niggers." But woe to an outsider doing such.

As far as my father was concerned, the usher might as well have been yelling, "Make way for the leper! Make way for the leper!" If the crowd had not been so thick, my father would have decked him.

The seats were in a terrible location behind and under the second deck. We would watch a batted ball go up into the air; then it would disappear behind the overhang, only to reappear in our view above the upper deck. My grandfather looked back at me and said:

"These are good seats," each time imploring me with his eyes to confirm it. The tickets were his gift to me, his crippled grandson. I kept nodding yes, and saying: "Yes, Grandpa, these are good seats."

Fortunately, I was allowed to glide right back in with my age group toward the end of the positive experience of Warm Springs. Being there had given me a good self-image, and a confident air.

I had been given lust lessons by mountaineer-sexologist J.D. Cobb. I had earned the right to dine in Georgia Hall. There had been the physical delight of practicing "Plus One" in tight embrace with sweet, soft therapist Bambi Cranmore.

Putting my new classmates at ease was relatively simple.

A group of boys approached me at recess time. Their leader grabbed his crotch and said, "You got anything to eat?"

"Self-service," was the proper ritualistic reply. The arcane argot of sodomy always has been part of the barbaric male teenage world. Familiarity with the natives' language proved useful.

"Hey, he's all right!" the leader of the pack exclaimed. With that, I was in like Flynn the first day—just one of the guys.

With the girls, acceptance came almost as quickly. I was a thin, sensitive-faced boy, and my plight no doubt pulled on young feminine heartstrings.

I had a note of mystery about me. I had traveled, and sounded intelligent beyond the confines of the St. Joseph seventh-grade classroom. Much of that was due to constant reading. So I got the girls' acceptance quickly, also. It was not very long before the acceptance of one girl was all that mattered.

Her name was Jacque. At 5-foot-2 and only 14, she had the body of a young-adult woman. She had short, dark brown hair, cut to frame her face. She was hazel-eyed and equipped with a heart-piercing smile. Think of Annette Funicello, the nationally known "Mouseketeer" who was the object of the lust of young American males at the time. Picture Annette with a better figure and smaller, finer facial features—smaller nose and mouth—and you will have a picture of Jacque.

She returned the overtures of affection; at least that was my strong impression for a number of years. I am not talking about great physical passion. In those years, I would have liked that. There simply was no place to be passionate. I had to settle for clandestine little hand-holding get-togethers in briefly empty classrooms, and nightly telephone calls. These few drops of water on a parched heart stoked my affection. It grew into intense and painful love.

The nuns whose task it was to try and civilize the young barbarians who had now accepted me were of the Society of Divine Providence, an order that originated in Germany. Headquartered in Pittsburgh, they were formidable-looking women. Most seemed to be cut from the same block of rugged black stone.

Their attitude toward me was summed up in a rather clandestine meeting early in the eighth grade with the high school principal, Sister De LaSalle.

The cafeteria was near the junior high school's entrance. It was 15 steps up to the eighth-grade room. While I was unsuspectingly dining on a sandwich of mom's meat loaf, the tall, ascetic-looking nun appeared in the classroom doorway. The high school principal made few visits to the junior high, so obviously something was afoot.

First, she handed me a small bottle that, she said reverently, held water from Lourdes, the French site where the Blessed Virgin Mary appeared to the young girl, Bernadette.

After telling me to take the water home and pray after making the sign of the cross using the water from Lourdes, Sister De LaSalle then said something that was disturbing.

"Jerry," she said in a conspiratorial whisper, "did you know that you can save souls by your pain and suffering? Just offer up your pain and suffering for people in need of God's grace."

Whoa, Nelly!

Pain and suffering? Here I was just starting to enjoy life again, and now this strange person garbed in black and a starched white covering framing her face with only hands showing below was saying that my suffering could save souls.

I had just marched through a bizarre hell. I was trying as hard as possible to be "normal" like the other kids. Her theme became a repetitive one in my life. It got under my skin, never to be dislodged.

As an adult, I would come grudgingly to accept Pope John Paul II's inspired explanation of the usefulness of suffering as spelled out in his biography "Witness to Hope." But there I was in my fourteenth year struggling to bust out of a body that would never quite do exactly what I asked it to do. Everything that I did was an attempt to show people that I could be as good as, or better, than the next kid.

As an eighth-grader, I was our school's entrant in the county spelling bee. The local newspaper gave a hint as to my emerging role:

"The contestants were reduced to four. Then the crowd favorite, Jerry Range, from Dover St. Joseph, failed. His word was 'placid,' and he paused after the first 'c', then added another 'c.' There were many moist eyes in the crowd." Misspelling the word "placid" was truly a harbinger of my adult life.

No day goes by without an interior skirmish: my fading wish to live in a useful body vs. the knowledge of melding with the Crucified Christ in the Eucharist—and where bread and wine in the hands of a priest become the actual body and blood of Christ.

I am a thoroughly human being, and some simple human comforts would be delightful: a trip to the bathroom with the daily newspaper's sports section in hand when nature calls instead of when the clock requires; blowing my nose without help; a stroll through a park as ducks and geese glide onto a lagoon during twilight.

Doubt remains a constant in my religiosity. Maybe that is what separates saints from sinners—the saint knows, the sinner hopes. And, by the way, have they made heaven accessible to wheelchairs?

A cripple like me dies, arrives in a wheelchair at the Pearly Gates, and looks up a flight of seemingly endless golden stairs.

St. Peter grabs the hotline: "Hey, we got another one of those problem types here. When are you guys gonna get that damn, uh, I mean that dang ramp built?"

There are people who believed that as a seriously crippled 14-year-old, I already had my ticket to Paradise punched. But cripples such as I drag dirty baggage along with us just as anyone else does.

What the world did not know about me was that an inner storm of hunger for erotica raged. Dad had a subscription to the magazine "Argosy." It had action-adventure stories, but sometimes it veered close to pornography. At age 14, I read anything I could get my hand on.

I had a hunger for the erotic and still do. Why else would I remember such tripe more than four decades later?

Paradoxically, when I was not scrounging for bits of erotica, I might be praying the rosary. The Knights of Columbus of Ohio gave me a plaque for the best essay titled, "What the Blessed Virgin Mary Means to Me."

There were enormous chunks of time. I filled them with steady reading. That included a slog through Tolstoy's enormous "War and Peace." I plowed through William Shirer's voluminous "History of the Third Reich." I devoured Alexander P. deSeversky's "Victory through Air Power," the blueprint for strategic aerial bombing in World War II. I was so enamored with flying that my parents gave me a subscription to "Flying" magazine.

My favorite book, "Reach for the Sky," was the biography of Douglas Bader, who as a Royal Air Force fighter pilot in 1931 crashed and lost both of his legs. Bader re-taught himself how to fly.

He did it so well that in 1940 when the Royal Air Force needed every experienced pilot it could find to defend against the German Luftwaffe, Bader was reinstated. He was given one of the famed

"Spitfire" fighters. With his artificial legs working the controls, Bader blasted dozens of German planes out of the English sky.

The man and his book inspired me. I envied his time in the sky.

"Jer," my father said on what promised to be another boring summer day, "how would you like to take a ride in an airplane?"

Dad had spent about $30 of his hard-earned money on a half-hour plane ride at the airport in neighboring New Philadelphia, the county seat. Dad drove me to Harry Cleaver Field. The little plane was a two-seater. Dad lifted me into the seat through the door under the wing.

For a kid who could not walk, churning above the earth at 180 mph was ecstasy. The pilot would yell over the roar of the engine, "Look, a strip mine down to the right!" Tuscarawas County, like surrounding counties, had strip mines on nearly every hill. From the air, a strip mine looked like someone had taken a giant penknife and had ripped a gouge in the green earth. We flew as far north as Canton, about 30 miles.

Thirty minutes was over before I could do as the poem said of the aviator: " . . . slipped the surly bonds of Earth . . . and reached out and touched the face of God."

When not reading my way through the Dover Public Library, I assumed the role of buffer between my mother and father.

"I just do not know what I am going to do with your mother, Jer. She is just unlivable," my father would say as we drove to a customer's house in the country to check on his need for a propane fill-up. My father sold propane gas and kitchen appliances. In the summer, I often accompanied him.

As she was setting the table or doing some other household chore, my mother would say, "Your father can be so hard to get along with. Sometimes, he will not speak about important things for days. I just do not know what to do with him."

As I had done with my father, I would simply nod and maybe mumble a noncommittal, "Yeah, well, uh huh." Like so many married couples, they needed someone to speak to about their relationship. Because of pride and the inability to say what was in their hearts, they turned to someone else for a listener. I was that listener.

Polio drove my father and me together in an intimate way that we never would have known had I not been crippled.

Every night, my father would lock the brakes of my wheelchair at the entry to the hallway in the middle of the house. Then he would slide me forward and lock my long-leg braces, put the silver crutches under my arms and pull me to a standing position.

For about 20 minutes, I would throw the right crutch forward followed by a forward swing of the left leg. Then the left crutch (which was strapped tightly to the totally paralyzed left arm) would be swung forward, followed by the forward move of the right leg. Right, left; left, right; right, left; left, right, down the hall.

At the end of the hall, with my father's hand hovering close to my belt, I would complete the pivot that would have me staring at my wheelchair 30 feet away. After catching my breath, I would begin the return trek. At the wheelchair, I would once again pivot 180 degrees and be lowered, exhausted and sweating, into the chair.

My father was my personal physical therapist and my personal nurse. He would lift me on and off the toilet, in and out of the tub, and in and out of bed. Our common language was sports, particularly baseball:

"The Indians are not going anywhere but down until they get some decent pitching," he would say.

"No," I would reply, "they need more hitting. Colavito can't carry that team all by himself!" It was an easy intimacy until my father lost his job in 1961.

For several years, he would say almost nightly, "I should go down to the basement and put a shotgun in my mouth and pull the trigger." My stomach would twist into knots, because I could see despair darken his face. I had no useful words of hope. The system my father had believed in had failed him. I could offer little but youthful banalities.

"Dad, don't say that kind of stuff, please. Something will happen, things will get better."

"Bullshit! Every time you think you're getting ahead, the world smacks you right in the face with a two-by-four!"

My mother had taken a job as a receptionist in a doctor's office. Maybe the suicide talk was only the venting of frustration. Maybe it was the expression of the sense of impotence men have when they cannot be the bread winner.

When we first moved into the house in 1958, my older brother Tom had practiced his sharp shooting by firing a .22-caliber rifle through a basement window at the neighbor's dog when it was on our lawn. The dog was not hit, but the police were called. That began a long-running feud in which we were not allowed to talk to our peers next door.

That was truly unfortunate. Next door there were three teenage sisters close in age. The three shapely young ladies became cheerleaders at Dover High School. In the summer, clad in T-shirts and flimsy shorts, they would practice their cartwheels and splits as I watched hungrily from the patio.

In the summer of 1957, I was light years removed from the Jerry Range of that August day in 1955, when I walked out of my sunny childhood in Erie, Pa.

Many believe that the older one is when a crippling event occurs, then the more difficult it is for a person to adjust to being immobilized.

They believe it is better to be born crippled than to be crippled later in life.

I believe that the more good memories a person has had before he is suddenly rendered physically immobile, the more likely it is that he can surmount the new difficulties. Our memory banks are storehouses of happy times, deeds and doings where we can retreat to reload our emotional guns and steel our psyches for tough times ahead.

One of the things I am going to ask God when I see Him is why I wasn't allowed two more weeks of physical normalcy. Would that have skewed the Cosmic Plan so awfully much?

With those extra two weeks, I could have played on that city championship Little League team back in '55. That would have been a lifetime memory worth going back to time and time again.

Thus, to say that a child is better off being born crippled than to be crippled at age 11 is to say life is not worth living to the fullest.

I had been taught at Warm Springs to charge full tilt into the fray with banners flying, and with sword unsheathed. That is how I re-entered "normal" life at St. Joseph Junior High School in 1957 at Dover, Ohio.

I was not yet an adult as the eighth grade flew by.

All the young men in the eighth grade had nuclear-powered hormones bouncing around inside us. Although I had made the rough rite of passage through the lingering vestiges of puberty, anything could set us off into uncontrollable bouts of mirth.

For instance, one day in Sister Huberta's eighth-grade classroom, we were reading about the rubber industry in Akron. The short, stout little nun ordered one of the boys to read aloud from the text.

Every time a young man would read the word "rubber" aloud, muffled laughter would erupt from the rest of us.

Disgusted, Sister then ordered another young man to read. The result was the same. I dreaded what was coming. She ordered me to read. Somehow, I managed to get through the text, but only with tears streaming down my contorted face.

She exclaimed to the girls who were segregated in one-half of the classroom: "I cannot understand why any young woman would want to share a bed with an uncouth, probably drunken man—and they all are, you know!"

Sister Huberta was only too glad to see us move on to high school.

There was a very old nun by the name of Sister Laurentine, a very gentle lady, who was nominally retired. However, there were only four nuns on the high school faculty, so Sister Luarentine was pressed into service to teach chemistry and typing.

Two of the young barbarians in my class actually sat at the top step of the 39 that Sister Laurentine had to climb. Periodically, she would stop to rest. My two classmates bet a quarter on which steps she would pause.

They were a rough, raw, and rowdy group. Thank God for football. It harnessed all that raw, post-pubescent energy.

Football dominated the fall in eastern Ohio. It still does. People in small towns that had small high schools not yet consolidated with others looked upon their football teams as their reason for existence. Football was not a sport. It was a life-and-death affair.

None of the schools in our county would schedule us. So we played schools in small towns in neighboring counties; towns like Navarre, Brewster, Beach City, East Canton, Danville. They all took special delight in beating Catholic schools.

We were 0-7-1 going into the game at Zanesville Bishop Rosecrans. The final game scheduled the next week would be against hated archrival Dennison St. Mary's, whose quarterback, Alex "Sandy" Bonvechio, would go on to quarterback Notre Dame. He is mentioned in the movie "Rudy." There was little hope of winning that game.

Rosecrans seemed our last chance at victory. To the surprise of everyone in the stadium, we were tied with the Bishops 0-0 at halftime. Then-Coach Joe LaScola walked over to me as his troops were filing into the locker room.

"Jerry, would you like to come in and say something to the guys?" he said. I was thrilled at the thought. I was not so thrilled at the smell of sweat, mud, and an over-used commode that hit me as I entered the locker room.

"Listen up, you guys," the coach said. "This guy may be crippled, but he is tough where it counts," he said pointing to his chest.

Entirely impromptu, I launched into my first pep talk:

"Guys, there might be nothing else in your life that will be as important as the next two quarters of football. Forget about anything else! Throw everything you have into the next two quarters. Do it for your girl friends. Do it for your parents. Do it for your school. Just do it! Do it! Win! Just win! Don't stop fighting, scratching, and clawing, you Ramblers, until the final whistle! Get out there and show them how a St. Joe football player fights!"

It sounds so hackneyed now, but the team members nearly

killed a young cripple in their efforts to get out the door and get after the opponent.

My heart was pounding. I had commanded the attention of those 35 or so muddy, bloody warriors. The rush of adrenaline gave me a sense of power and strength I never knew I had.

We won, 14-7. In front of the squad, the coach gave me the game ball. It is on my bookshelf 48 years later, with the names signed by the players fading badly.

Being made to feel useful would continue for three more years because of another man. Art Teynor would be the first of many mentors who would give me a lift up to the next rung on life's ladder.

We first met in spring of 1959 in the school gym. His sturdy body, about 5-foot-10, was like a solid slab of corn-fed beef one might find in his native Bucyrus on the western Ohio plain. He had a ruddy complexion on his square Irish face.

The Coach took my hand in his paw that was more like a thick piece of ham than a hand. He looked me in the eye, and said, "I need you."

He was a gruff man with a mushy heart. He genuinely liked teenagers, which was no mean feat.

He and I began a bond that spring day in 1959 that would grow through the years despite the separation of miles and vastly different lives. He pushed me to excel academically. An ardent Democrat, he anointed me as the class liberal. He would incite near riots by playing me off against Bill Krantz, the class Republican.

He made me feel useful by having me keep statistics for the football team. He made me the public announcer at basketball games. He gave me the job of official scorer for the baseball team.

For three critical years, he gave my self-image a huge boost. For instance, in my senior year he made it clearly known to the football players that a trophy honoring the top defensive player would be given based on the tackle chart that I would keep on the sidelines.

After the game, at least half a dozen players would make a beeline to me to find out how many tackles I had awarded each player. Then they would lobby for more tackles to be added to their total, and for other tackles to be deducted from other players' totals. Secure in my power, I laughed at their entreaties.

The hardest thing for me to deal with in my high school years was my sexuality. Our religion taught that the sex drive before marriage must be harnessed and held in check. Intercourse was, of course, out of the question for a Catholic teenager.

Still, sexuality can find many innocent outlets—holding hands, sitting together and just talking, a short car trip to get an ice cream cone, an occasional peck on the cheek, cuddling at a dance or at a chaperoned party.

Of course, there was sublimation; that is, the letting off of the sexual tension in rough physical activity—running, swimming, playing football, basketball, or other sports.

It is hard to sublimate when one can barely move.

All those things were denied me, not only because I was physically disabled, but also because I had picked the wrong girl to become infatuated with, and as I grew older, to love.

A number of boys let me know they resented my taking Jacque "out of action." While I might have had something to do with Jacque's being "out of action," there was no "action" between us.

There was no hand-holding, no peck on the cheek, no hug, no innocent kiss, no cuddling at parties, at post-game sock hops, or in a car. There was only a nightly phone call, and occasional chats in briefly empty classrooms.

Our relationship was what the word "platonic" was made for.

For four years, as we grew toward manhood and womanhood, she had done nothing that I can think of to discourage me from falling deeper and deeper in love.

Then I was body-slammed in the school hallway in November of our senior year:

"Jerry," she said, "I am going away to Pittsburgh to be a nun as soon as we graduate. We should start to bring things to an end."

I blurted out: "But I love you, and I thought that you loved me."

"I guess that I love God more than I love you," she said.

She allowed me fewer and fewer phone calls. She did agree to go with me to our final prom. We doubled with my friend and his date. After the prom, post-prom, and early breakfast, he took his date home. Then on the way to Jacque's home, she consented to a kiss as we sat in the back seat.

The first kiss, the last kiss.

After the chaste touch of lips, I said in a rush of gratitude, "Thank you, and thank your mother for having you."

"Oh, don't be silly," she said. Her words were like being hit in the face with ice-cold water. Then we were at her house, she was out of the car, and, practically speaking, out of my life.

Strangely, her last words to me came on our final day in high school. At the final bell, she came close to me, leaned on the front of my wheelchair, stared directly into my eyes and said, "Now you get that law degree like I told you!"

The final time I saw her came on a day in June as I waited in the car while my father was in school getting transcripts to send to colleges. To my left across the side street was the nuns' residence. She came out the door, saw me, but did not say hello, or even wave. Her car was parked in front of ours. She got in her car and drove out of my life.

It would be a distortion to say that my high school years were spent doing nothing but worrying over Jacque. I was class president a few years, president of the student council, and chief pep-rally speaker.

When I was a senior, I worked at the local rip-and-read radio station on Sunday nights: "This is WJER, 1450 on your radio dial; the voice and choice of Tuscarawas County," I would say into the microphone.

My fondest memory lives on in a plaque. The Coach gave it to me at the football banquet when I was a sophomore. Its simple wording encapsulates all I felt for that tiny school of 140 students and its big-hearted coach:

"Jerry Range. St. Joseph's most loyal fan. 1960."

Though human in their foibles, the nuns were hard-working

women who believed passionately in educating school children. Sister DeLaSalle, Sister Anselma, Sister Dolorita, the gentle and pretty Sister Teresa, who taught me three years of Latin, and poor little Sister Laurentine, who deserved a quiet retirement, all did extraordinary work.

They poured Latin, German, geometry, algebra, trigonometry, pre-calculus, chemistry, Principles of Democracy, English, history, and religion into students like me. When I left that tiny high school, I was ready to compete at one of the nation's fine land grant institutions, the University of Illinois.

I said goodbye to a school I loved, and to a coach who made me feel part of the process.

Yes, a beautiful young woman had stung my heart, and the memory of her would bother me for decades. But the buoyancy of youth just would not let me sink too deeply into despondency. Events that summer were moving fast.

I sensed a good future rushing toward me. I wanted to meet it head-on. I had passed the test of operating in an able-bodied world. I had conquered the problems of personal hygiene—washing, getting on and off a toilet.

By using the leverage techniques taught at Warm Springs, I had mastered the problems of dressing and transferring in and out of my wheelchair into bed and back into the chair.

In bed, I would lie on my left side, drop my left leg down alongside the braked wheelchair, grab it with my right arm, and with a rolling motion, swing out over the floor and up to a sitting position. Then after repositioning the chair at an angle on my left, I would lift my left foot onto the left front wheel, reach under the leg and pull a sliding board onto the bed. With a few more tugs and a bit more leveraging, I was in the chair.

To pull up my pants over my butt, I could lift up my hips by hooking my shoulder blades on the posture panel in the chair.

Socks were started onto my feet by leaning down and placing them over the front portion of the foot. The left foot stayed on the foot platform. I would place the right leg over the lower, front portion of the chair arm and tug till the sock came up.

I didn't think. I just did what was necessary.

It took every ounce of physical and emotional energy simply to get through an average day on the campus of the University of Illinois. The same would be true of most of the days of the next 25 years.

I got to the University of Illinois by way of Georgia. I had been accepted at John Carroll University, a small Catholic college run by the Jesuits in a Cleveland suburb. I failed to tell JCU that I was severely crippled. A recruiter for the school gave a presentation at St. Joe. After his talk, my parents wheeled me up to him.

I told him I had been accepted at John Carroll. A week later, I received a letter from John Carroll virtually begging me to enroll elsewhere.

The state of Ohio said that it would foot the entire bill to put me through a state university—if I agreed to have an attendant live with me. The idea was distasteful, but we accepted what seemed to be the inevitable. I enrolled at Bowling Green State University.

We made an outpatient trip to Warm Springs in June, and while there, we stopped in the office of the staff psychologist, the gracious Grace Marie Freyman. She had been enormously encouraging in my days at Warm Springs. She had taught me not to limit my dreams.

I mentioned that while I was not happy about having to live with an attendant, I reluctantly had agreed to attend Bowling Green.

"Have you heard of the University of Illinois?" she said.

"It's in the Big Ten," I replied. "That's about all I know about the school."

She explained that Illinois was the only university in the country in those days to accept large numbers of handicapped students and integrate them into the student body. The emphasis, she said, was on self-reliance.

We were excited. "Would you like to talk to the program's director, Dr. Timothy Nugent?" she asked me. I thought she meant she would write him on my behalf, and I would call him from home. So, I said yes.

She called him immediately, and handed me the phone.

Nugent's dynamism knew no bounds, including geographical realities. I told him that we lived in eastern Ohio. "Can you detour by way of Champaign-Urbana?" he asked. I put the question to my father, who rapidly did some financial and geographical calculations.

"Tell him yes," Dad said.

Three days and 800 miles later, we were seated across a desk from a man who, we thought, was either the world's greatest con artist or the world's most enthusiastic and positive thinker.

Dr. Timothy J. Nugent, a physical therapist by trade, had the spell-binding appeal of "The Music Man's" Prof. Harold T. Hill and an unflagging belief in a righteous cause—he believed that crippled young men and women in his program could go on to succeed in life.

He explained that he had to take in-state (Illinois) students first until August 15. After that, he said he could consider out-of-state students such as myself.

"Go home," he said, "have your high school principal send your transcripts, and stay close to a phone." It rang on August 17. Dr. Nugent said I was accepted—conditionally.

"If you want to come," he said, "you will be in the first group of severely handicapped students—quadriplegics—that we have ever enrolled. We need to see if you can survive in a dormitory. Can you be here in seven days?"

"Dad, can we be at Champaign-Urbana in seven days?" I asked.

"Why not?" Dad said rhetorically. "We've come this far, so let's play out the string."

Horace Greeley would have been proud. An excited young man went west seven days later.

End of Chapter 4

CHAPTER 5

"On the Prairie with Dr. Tim, Bucky, Gene"

It took me only two days to convince Dr. Nugent and his staff that I could survive in a dormitory on campus.

But I was painfully homesick. When my parents left the dormitory room that was to be my "testing place," I cried bitterly. On the night of the second day of my "testing," I called my parents.

"Dad, I just can't take this being alone out here. It hurts too much. I want to come home," I said. We talked a while longer. Finally, my father said, "If that is what you really want—to come home—I will come to get you. But first I think you should talk to Dr. Nugent."

I was unhappy with that advice, but I agreed to do it.

On the morning of the third day on campus, I went to the director's secretary and asked if I could see him. She went into his office, and immediately beckoned me to enter.

Dr. Nugent leaned back in his chair behind his desk with his fingers locked behind his head topped by thick, wavy bronzed-colored hair, studying me through his wire-rimmed glasses.

Between long sobs I managed to say, "I cannot stand it. I have to get back to my parents. It just hurts too much."

When I was done, he leaned forward, propped his elbows on the desk, clasped his hands together and pointed his two thick forefingers at me like weapons. His words slammed into me like machine-gun bullets:

"We do not need cry babies like you around here! Go home to your Mommy and Daddy, you sniveling little son of a bitch! There are plenty of others who would be glad to take your place."

"Here," he said, "you can even use my phone to make the long-distance call." He angrily shoved the phone across the desk at me.

I felt as if a heavyweight fighter had just smashed my face. My mind was reeling. I was stunned.

I felt my face turning bright red.

I switched the electric wheelchair to high speed, spun, and sped out of his office.

"That son of a bitch," I said to myself when I got back to my dorm room, "is not going to run me out of the University of Illinois."

Tim Nugent's savvy ploy had worked perfectly.

Four years later, at the Rehabilitation Center banquet at homecoming, I learned that my family had come to grips with the same crisis. The Rehab Center always asked the parent of a senior to give a talk. My father spoke in 1966.

He recalled that day in 1962 when they began the 500-mile drive back to eastern Ohio:

"We were driving east on I-74. I looked over at my wife, and saw that she was crying. I looked back over my shoulder at my son Jim, and saw that he was crying. I looked in the rearview mirror, and saw that I was crying."

After the laughter had died down, he continued: "I pulled off onto the shoulder of the highway and asked my wife and son, 'Should we go back and get Jerry?' I said that if we did, he would probably be losing his last chance at an independent life. Eventually, we all stopped crying and agreed that we should go on back home to Ohio without him."

The Rehab Center offered private testing for those who could not write, speak, or see; bus service for everyone enrolled in the program, and the ability to get the site of a class changed if it were in an inaccessible room. In addition, there was physical therapy that we were required to take in lieu of the university's requirement of two years of physical education.

One of the nicest things about the Rehab Center was a guy named Joe Konitzky. Joe was the assistant director of the program, and often was in charge because Dr. Nugent made many overseas trips as a consultant in the rehabilitation field.

Joe's door was always open. A student could roll in at any time and unburden himself or herself. Joe was a great listener, and his replies given in soft tones made you feel better because of his gentle, reassuring air.

He was tall, with short-cropped hair—physically the opposite of Nugent. Emotionally, he was also the counterpoint to the director. Nugent was brash, even abrasive, and he always operated at full throttle. Joe's advice was always understated. For me, he was a great resource of encouragement, and a greater friend.

The Rehab students spared no one their savage humor. If a person could survive that no-holds-barred verbal pummeling, he could survive any kind of verbal harassment in the "real" world.

Kerry Baymond had a degenerative neuromuscular disease. He was dying. He was trying to beat the clock by getting his degree before death got him. He refused all help. Sometimes it would take him as long as ten minutes to roll from a classroom building to the bus.

All the while, Rehab students would be shouting out the bus windows, "Come on you damned cripple, I want to get to supper on time!" or, "Baymond, you are so fucking crippled, you make us all look bad!"

Kerry and I became friends. As my four years sped by, his strength rapidly ebbed, forcing him to take lighter academic loads. He persevered in his quest for a diploma in finance. He got it a year after I graduated.

He died a month after getting the degree. Was it worth the fight? Was he a winner? Damn right he was.

Beyond the rough-and-tumble humor, there were a number of themes emerging early on for me.

I learned it was okay to enjoy learning for learning's sake.

But as much as I came to love that magnificent university with its long green quadrangle, life was a daily battle just to survive physically and emotionally. It took all my energy to keep going. On most days during the school week, I felt like I was walking in hip-deep mud or chewing metal. The physical demands were exhausting my reserves.

There were gorgeous girls everywhere, but none of them had my name sewed on her blouse. It was like living in a cloistered monastery with voluptuous women marching up and down the hallway at all hours of the day.

I was learning to plan things very carefully. A crucial reason was my constant fear of urination at the wrong time in the wrong place.

As I grew into adulthood, that fear would shape my days.

An entire new world opened up to me as I took courses in the humanities, history, political science, English literature, and geography. I quickly learned how to tailor class schedules to my needs. The first semester saw me going to Rhetoric 101 at 8 a.m. and German at 4 p.m. I quickly dispensed with that kind of schedule the next semester.

The high points were very high, and the lows were as bad as it could get in those first four months. When I came out of my world history class with a big red "A-" on my first college test paper, I knew I could compete at a Big Ten university.

On the other hand, one bitterly cold early December day near the end of my first semester, I was cutting across the quadrangle in a snowstorm to get to my German class at 4 in the already-darkening afternoon. My early-model electric wheelchair chose that moment to simply stop.

There I was, in 20-degree weather with snow piling upon me as if I were a statue. I sat there for maybe ten minutes before a helpful "AB" (able-bodied person) came along and offered help. He pushed me to my German class. Another student pushed me to the bus stop.

To get to the 8 a.m. class in my first semester, my routine would be: (1) Up at 6 a.m. with 45 minutes to get out of bed and to dress; (2) ten minutes to transfer from the manual wheelchair to the electric; (3) 25 minutes to brush my teeth, wash my face, shave, and comb my hair; (4) ten minutes to get into a jacket or coat (I wore the lightest winter jacket in which I could get by in the prairie winters); (5) seven or eight minutes to gather my books and notebooks; (6) two or three minutes to get to the bus stop near my dorm 20 minutes before the hour; (7) five minutes to get to class from the drop-off site.

I rarely took off my winter coat in a classroom, because it would take too long to get it back on and I did not want to risk missing the bus.

There was only one electric-repair shop in Champaign-Urbana that would work on those early models of electric wheelchairs. This was in the days when there were no solid-state electronics. Every time I called, a huge man well over six feet tall and weighing at least 350 pounds would come strolling down the lane to my dormitory in his bib overalls to take the wheelchair to the repair shop.

Once after he had returned the chair, there was something rattling in the control box. One of the guys on my floor was majoring in electrical engineering. He had long wanted to get into the innards of my wheelchair. I gave him the go-ahead.

He opened the control box, and out fell a dried piece of beef. We surmised that the rotund repairman had been eating his lunch—a beef sandwich—over the open control box and a piece of beef had slid out from between the pieces of bread and had fallen into the box.

In the crippled business, beggars could not be choosers.

Learning was fun. I chose a humanities class for my second semester. The professor was about 5-foot-7, and was nervous lecturing to students. Nevertheless, his lectures about our readings from Homer's "Iliad," and the "Odyssey," the "Golden Ass of Apulius," the writings of St. Augustine, those of St. Thomas Aquinas, and the "Canterbury Tales," to name a few, were spellbinding.

I sat up front on the right side slightly behind the professor. The little lecturer's hands would be clasped tightly to the podium, and he was constantly raising himself on the balls of his feet, putting his feet back down on the floor, and repeating the process.

In the back of the room there were three or four idiots who carried on an annoying conversation for several class periods.

Finally, the little professor summoned up his courage. His arms were shaking as he clung tightly to the podium. He said: "There are people here who want to learn. You ruffians are denying them the opportunity they paid for. If you cannot be quiet, please leave."

Several did as we cheered and jeered loudly. I so enjoyed that semester of humanities that I took another semester's worth taught by the little professor.

In my first semester, I did not see my parents from late August until Christmas vacation.

I spent Thanksgiving vacation together in a common dormitory with foreign students and those from far-distant U.S. locations. I was lonely, bored, and of course homesick.

My father said, "Jer, I can't drive 1,000 miles round-trip and then four days later turn around and do it again."

Out of necessity, I was growing up very fast.

When my father came out on Dec. 19 to take me home for Christmas vacation, the Midwest was experiencing one of its coldest Decembers on record. We spent the night at the Holiday Inn. We awoke to blowing snow, a temperature of 20 degrees below zero Fahrenheit, and winds of 25 mph. My dad wrapped me in blankets, because even with the car heater turned up full-blast, it was still bitterly cold in the car.

"If we make it home in one piece, this will be a hell of a family story," my father said.

"Yeah, if hypothermia doesn't get me first," I said through the chattering of my teeth.

As we came up over a rise in the road in rural Indiana, there was a horse standing stiff as a board in our lane. My father managed to whip around the horse's south end and get past him without doing damage to car or horse.

Relaxing, my father stopped at an intersection a quarter-mile down the road. The car went into a 360-degree spin. We ended up in a ditch. With the help of other drivers, we were able to get on our way.

At Thanksgiving time of my sophomore year, I was looking through the university's student directory. I found names from my area of eastern Ohio. I hit pay dirt on the fourth call.

"Yeah, I can take you home," the guy said. "I live in the Youngstown area and I have one place left in my car. If you want it, you can have the space. You three guys share the cost of the gasoline."

A young man showed up at my dormitory door, and said, "Your magic carpet has arrived." I held my suitcase on my feet and he pushed me outside.

My heart sank when I saw a rusty, dented Volkswagen Beetle that probably had seen service on the Russian front in World War II.

Since I had been the third person to call, I was relegated to the back seat. It would have been simple to lift me into the front seat. But caller No. 1 would not offer his seat, and we're talking of college-aged young men here—not often known for the application of logic. So the trio got me horizontal in mid-air and stuffed me through the one door on the driver's side onto the back seat.

"Seat" was a very generous term for the fabric-covered board upon which I sat for 11 hours as we meandered through rural Indiana and across Ohio, often in pea-soup fog.

Finally we reached Massillon, where my father picked me up about 1 a.m. By then, my brain was no longer in communication with my rear end. Three days later the driver called and said that our buddies had canceled out, and the front seat was mine for the return trip.

We met in downtown Massillon, and I traveled in luxury in the deeply padded front seat. About 40 miles from the university, the driver lost control and we spun off the road into a deep ditch.

Six young males simply picked up the VW beetle with me inside, and carried it up to the road. The driver got in, and off we went.

That was the end of my 500-mile automobile trips at vacation time. Somehow we cobbled together the money, and I began to fly on Ozark Airlines into Chicago's O'Hare airport, where I would get a Northwest Orient or United Airlines flight to the Akron-Canton Airport.

A week before my first flight home, I read about a plane skidding off the runway at Akron-Canton. It was a United flight. United always boarded me first, and put me in the front row of first-class seats.

A loud-mouthed guy in a cheap suit and a penchant for poor timing said to the stewardess in Chicago, "Any more planes slide off the runway at Akron?" There was deathly silence in the plane as people stared daggers at him.

On the return flight from Akron, there was only a handful of passengers up front. Our stewardess passed out dinner trays and drinks. She then sat down next to me and helped me cut the food and sip the coffee. She had a German accent, and she splendidly filled out her blue stewardess uniform. She had blue eyes with flecks of hazel in them. We talked all the way to Chicago.

Another 500 miles in the air and I would have been hopelessly in love.

As I sat on the seat up front on the United flight at Easter vacation, a little old man in a rumpled overcoat got on at O'Hare in Chicago.

"Oh, God," I said to myself, "I hope he doesn't sit next to me." The little old man looked down and said, "Is this seat taken?" I answered no. He sat down.

We said little until the stewardess served dinner. With only one half-good arm and a hand that was not totally functional, I needed to be up to a table to have the leverage needed to cut the meat and to lift the coffee cup to my lips.

After only a minute, the old man said, "May I help you with your dinner?" I reluctantly nodded yes. He cut up the meat, and lifted the coffee cup to my mouth. He was gentle, considerate, and kind.

After the meal, he asked me where I had come from and what my destination was. I launched into a 10-minute dissertation on my life with all my penny-ante hopes and dreams. Finally, I realized that I had not even asked his name or his destination.

"Oh," he said, "I am going to Kent State University to deliver a lecture, and then I have to go on to Paris to give another lecture. From there, it's on to Prague, Czechoslovakia."

"What is your name and what you do?" I said.

"Oh," he said matter-of-factly, "my name is R. Buckminster Fuller. My friends call me 'Bucky.' I would like you to call me that."

"What do you do?" I said stupidly.

"Well," he said, "let me try to show you one thing we are working on." With that, he took a "Time" magazine that I had been paging through, and in the margin of one page drew a small, inverted semicircular thing that looked like the skeleton of an igloo.

"We call it a geodesic dome. It is being used in a number of ways, such as in radar, and we think we can apply the design to many other uses." He then took a little penknife, cut out the little picture and gave it to me.

We chatted amiably for the rest of the flight, and said a warm goodbye at Akron. When I greeted my mother and father, I showed my mother the little picture.

She said, "I think you've just sat next to a very important person." The next day she went to her new job at the Dover Public Library. When she came home, she had a biography of one of the great minds of the 20th century.

R. Buckminster Fuller, inventor of the geodesic dome that had been the home for the U.S. exhibit at the Montreal world's fair, had cut my beef and had served me my coffee. He had been one of the innovators of radar. One of his current projects was a proposal for insect-resistant wheat to give farmers in Third World countries greatly increased yields.

As luck would have it, "Time" magazine the next week had on its cover a picture of Fuller. "Time" called R. Buckminster Fuller one of the greatest minds of the 20th century. His home base was an institute at Southern Illinois University in Carbondale.

I had sat next to greatness. It did not rub off.

That particular spring I had to declare a major. I went to my academic adviser. "I am interested in being a social studies major to teach history in high school," I said half-heartedly.

He looked over my transcripts and said, "I think you'll need a few semesters of psychology, and that might mean you will have to spend a little more time in school."

Like most college students, I did not know how good I had it—life on a college campus is the best of all possible worlds this side of the hereafter. I wanted to get out of college as soon as possible, so I went over to the College of Communications and enrolled in radio news.

As an elective, I chose a rather interesting-sounding course called "Contemporary Affairs." It was a two-hour course.

"How significant can that be?" I thought.

When I came back for my junior year, I plunged into radio news writing and affiliated courses. I did some on-the-air work on the university's FM station, WILL. I also started attending the "insignificant" two-hour course called "Contemporary Affairs."

A large bear of a man walked into a basement classroom of Gregory Hall, and wrote on the blackboard: "Journalism 201, Contemporary Affairs."

"Anyone who does not want to read a lot of newspapers, y'all leave now," the man with an unruly shock of red hair said. Several people walked out. About a dozen of us remained.

"My name is Gene Graham, and I am going to turn you into people who will be eager to know what is going on in the outside world far beyond the borders of this campus," he said. "I am going to make you hunger and thirst for news."

Graham identified himself as a former reporter and editorial writer for the Nashville "Tennesseean," and most recently a Nieman Fellow at Harvard University. He was beginning his first semester as a journalism instructor at Illinois.

He had won a Pulitzer Prize at the "Tennesseean." His series of editorials had chronicled the progress of the Baker V. Carr case, the so-called "one-man, one-vote" case. It paved the way for, among other things, blacks to gain full voting rights in the South.

Graham had written a book on the case called, "The Roundheads and the Levelers." Before becoming an editorial writer,

Graham had been shot at as a reporter covering mining strikes in Western Kentucky.

His rumpled coat, shirt, and tie seemed to be at war with his body. It made him seem very human and approachable. It quickly became apparent that he had a genuine interest in students. He "adopted" me, for reasons known only to him.

His teaching technique was to select a current event, and then go back and lay the historical context. We frequently read parts of the four Chicago papers and parts of the two St. Louis newspapers. He demanded lots of old-fashioned hard work. He was cut from rough cloth, but his intellect was deep and subtle.

He took the class up to Springfield, the Illinois capital, to hear Chicago's political "boss," Mayor Richard Daley, speak to a joint session of the legislature. My electric wheelchair blew a fuse. So Graham pushed the heavy chair and me around all day.

Because of him, I had changed my major to newspaper journalism.

"Jeery," he said in that Tennessee twang, "I don't mind given 'yer journalism career a start, but I sure as hell wish it wasn't so danged hard to git it goin'."

Graham was tough on his students, and not the least bit shy about embarrassing someone who made a serious faux pas.

When I took his advanced reporting class, I did a story on the Rehab Center. While I was interviewing Dr. Nugent, he asked if he could see a rough draft of my story. I agreed.

I talked about my story in Graham's class, and innocently mentioned that I had let Nugent read it first before turning it in. Graham severely rebuked me as the rest of the class listened.

"Jeery," he said, "never, and I mean never, let anyone read your story—other than your editor—before it's published." There were murmurs of approval. That lesson was burned into my psyche. I did not have to learn that lesson twice.

I had failed my mentor. I vowed never to do so again.

I fleshed out my education with a minor in history and heavy doses of American and English literature. For three years, I was the prototypical "grind." My only non-academic interest that I satisfied was sports. No matter how cold the weather, I never missed a football game in four years at mammoth Memorial Stadium. I saw every home basketball game in Assembly Hall.

I was hungry to be close to a young lady. No "AB" young woman ever responded to one of my overtures. For three years, I had overlooked a feminine resource close at hand.

There were a number of cute girls in wheelchairs. Early in my senior year, I called one and asked her if she would like to see an on-campus play. I was dumbfounded when she said, "What took you so long? We were all wondering when you would ask one of us to go out," she said.

Her name was Barbara Black. She was from Greencastle, Ind. She was one of the most delicate-looking girls I had ever seen. She was the first girl from the Rehab Center to pledge a sorority. She had raven-black, short-cropped hair framing a pink face that had a small straight nose and naturally red lips. She had flashing green eyes.

After the play, we went to the Illini Union, the student center, for something to eat. "A lot of girls in the Rehab program have often wondered why you never asked any of them out. I am honored to be the first," she said with a sweet smile that made me gulp.

As we were heading back to her dorm, I apologized for making her do so much wheeling. She was a good soldier and said that she "needed the exercise."

Outside her dorm, my reward for making her the first Rehab date of Jerry Range was a long, lingering series of soft kisses. Too many things intervened for a romance to bloom. But I kissed my way through half a dozen or so of the "pretty" girls in the Rehab program that final academic year.

I sold a story about the Rehab Center to the "Plain Dealer" in Cleveland. They ran it in the Sunday magazine. At Easter time, I had two interviews. One was with the Lorain "Journal," a paper run by a friend from Dover. Lorain is about 30 miles west of Cleveland. The other was with the "Plain Dealer."

I had hoped for an interview at the "Beacon Journal" in Akron. But the managing editor replied to my job inquiry this way: "We would like to meet with you, but our elevator is currently being repaired."

I had received many brush-offs, but that was the most clumsy and most stupid. It was as least as stupid as the question by the representative of a chain called Lindsay-Schaub newspapers. One of their representatives asked me, "How do you get on the toilet?" His companion rolled his eyes in embarrassment. I looked at the idiot questioner and said, "Sometimes fast, and sometimes slow."

Lorain offered $90 a week. My department head had mentioned to me that he had an acquaintance at the "Plain Dealer." Apparently, when I told him that I was going to interview with the "Plain Dealer," he contacted his acquaintance.

Before I could even make my pitch at my interview in the "PD" offices, I was offered a job on the copy desk at the "PD" for $103 a week with a 7 percent night differential raising it to $111.

It was no contest. Our friend at the Lorain paper was angry, but how could I pass up the extra money and the prestige of working for Ohio's largest paper? I accepted the "PD's" offer on the spot.

I was to begin work on July 1, 1966—forty-six days shy of a full eleven years after the crippling on Aug. 15, 1955. It had been quite a trip, but the journey was really only beginning.

End of Chapter 5

CHAPTER 6

"Of Lunatics and Would-be Lovers"

I left a lot of old baggage on the campus of the University of Illinois after graduation in June 1966. Long gone was the pining for high-school love, Jacque. That flame had flickered out about the time I became a journalism student in my junior year. Gone also were the quick and easy floods of tears.

The Rehab program at Illinois had provided a four-year breathing space, a chance to move from sheltered high school graduate to the doorway of physically independent adulthood. It had been a tough, draining fight that left me emotionally brittle and vulnerable.

For the first four days on the "Plain Dealer" copy desk, I was being studied from about 15 feet away by a tall, thin, bony man with a gray pallor. He sat wearing an old-fashioned green eye shade on his head casting a sickly glow over his face. He sometimes sat with his feet propped up on the desk while he edited the paper copy in midair. At other times, he slumped over leaning on one bony elbow at the far corner of the U-shaped copy desk.

Although in his late 40s, he looked older, especially when he pushed his upper or lower dentures out of his mouth. Few ventured near. Even the bosses gave him a wide berth.

I was nervous enough in my first days on the job. My stomach was churning, and my heart was pounding. I was wound tighter than the strings on a symphonic violin. And this human vulture was sizing me up like his next meal.

On the fourth night of my newspaper career, the bony hawk-like man uncoiled to his full 6-foot-2 height and walked around the U-shaped copy desk heading straight toward me. I froze as if 10 rifles were pointed at me, and someone had just said, "Ready, aim . . . ."

"Welcome to the copy desk, kid," he yelled, although he was standing only a foot away. All noise stopped. Everyone in the newsroom listened. "This is where they put the losers, boozers, and snoozers, the has-beens and the never-wases. I'm a has-been, and you're a never-was." Then he turned on his heel and stomped out the door to go to the cafeteria. The noise in the newsroom resumed.

That was my real introduction to big-city journalism. I was too stunned to reply. The man's name was John Metcalf, and he was certifiably on the edge of lunacy. The dozen or so other copy editors kept their distance. The next night when I arrived at 5, he said, "Here, kid, you can bunk next to me. Since you got your own chair, I'll even get rid of this one for you." He gave the rolling chair a mighty shove and it crashed into the wall ten feet behind him.

He was the most abnormal person I had ever met. I had spent eleven years trying to get back to "normal." Yet I was drawn to him like a tornado to a trailer park.

I thought that I had been hired as a fledgling journalist. As the first week neared its end, I felt like the rookie patient in an insane asylum where the patients were trying to make as much noise as possible.

Phones rang incessantly, people cursed and shouted at one another. Constantly the yell, "Boy!" rang throughout the large, messy room. There were 12 copy boys whose main job seemed to be keeping reporters and editors supplied with full cups of coffee. Their true function was to keep news copy flowing from reporters to editors, and to go on "art chases." When someone was murdered or killed in an accident, a copy boy was assigned to go get the person's picture.

There was a large black copy boy by the name of Earl. One night he offered to get a company car and take me home, even though that meant he would have to venture into the west side of

Cleveland. At that time the west side was all white. We headed for the high-level bridge far above the spot where the Cuyahoga River empties into Lake Erie. The car stopped dead in the speed lane. Earl had not checked the gas gauge. I expected to be killed by a car going 80 mph slamming into us.

A police car pulled up behind us. "What the hell are you doing over here, boy?" one of the white officers asked Earl. They pushed us several hundred yards to an off-ramp that went down under the freeway. There I sat expecting to be mugged or murdered while very black Earl trudged through white west side Cleveland looking for an open gas station at 1 a.m. It took him an hour to return with a can of gas. He never again offered to take me home.

For many years to come, Metcalf would be my mentor in newspapering and in the absurd side of life. Every evening when I reported for duty at 5, he would say, "Well, kid, we're one day closer to the end." He smoked foul-smelling cigars. When he finished one, he would simply throw it on the floor. There were pits all over the linoleum floor. One copy editor was always so drunk that he could not find his way to the men's room. Another copy editor, a man who became a recluse, always wore dark glasses and when he stood up and walked, the pills in the bottles in his pants jingled. Another would doze off every evening about 11. Quitting time was roughly 12:30 a.m.

"Has the Cleveland 'Plain Dealer' hired me," I wondered, "or have I been sent to Dante's fifth level of hell?"

My parents lived 80 miles south of Cleveland. After graduation they had taken me to Cleveland to find a wheelchair-accessible apartment. Someone directed us to the "Gold Coast" of Lakewood, the first suburb west of Cleveland. Along the shore of Lake Erie in Lakewood were six or seven high-rise apartment buildings.

There we found Winton Place, which was a posh 30-story apartment building with a huge blue script "W" on its roof. The architect had included one entire column—511 through 3011—of studio apartments. There was an expensive restaurant called Pier W that jutted out over Lake Erie 50 feet below. It was accessible to Winton Place residents by a private entrance.

For $160 a month, I rented apartment 2711. For that $160, I got one large room, a kitchenette, a dressing area with a closet, and a large bathroom. I also got a view of downtown Cleveland seven miles east.

In the bottom of the building was a party room free to residents, a barber shop, and a beauty shop. There was a life-guarded indoor pool. There were two levels in the underground garage. I moved in during the final weekend of June.

"Well, Jer," my father said, "I guess this is what it was all for." My mother said, "Call us for anything at any time." She gave me a kiss on the cheek, and with that they left me alone in a metropolitan area of 1.7 million people.

There was a knot in my throat, but no tears. Somewhere in college, the water works had gone dry.

"Remember," my mother had said, "register at the nearest Catholic church." I nodded yes, but I had stopped going to Mass early in my senior year back at the university. I did not consider myself agnostic. I simply was not practicing my faith.

My faith had gone dormant at a time of major upheaval in the Catholic Church. As I understand it, it was three or four years after that time of upheaval called Vatican II that Jacque, the high school girl I had once loved, left the convent for civilian life.

When I got to Cleveland in 1966, I called a girl by the name of Jeannemarie. She was the sister of one of those four of us who had been tested in 1962 for our ability to live in a dormitory. Her brother's name was Paul. Paul and I both made it into the dorms. However, he left Illinois after one academic year. He had introduced me to his sister on campus before his family returned to Cleveland.

During my four years on campus, she and I corresponded. When I got to Cleveland, she was a senior nursing student at a large school of registered nursing.

I called her soon after I got to Cleveland. By taxi, I took her to fancy restaurants and to the on-the-road productions of Broadway plays. One was "On a Clear Day You Can See Forever," starring Van Johnson and Linda Lavin.

I was rewarded a number of times outside the student nurses' residences with warm good-night kisses. One night on the way back to my tiny apartment in the sky, I told the cabbie, "I think that beautiful girl and I are on our way to something special."

"Good luck, buddy," he said, "I wish ya luck." When she graduated from nursing school in the spring, I was invited to the celebration. Her brother's friend took me to the ceremony. Then we went to a celebration at her home in Cleveland Heights, an upscale suburb in the eastern hills above Cleveland.

I was alone in the library. I could see the front door. The doorbell rang. Jeannemarie opened the door. A man in his late 20s or early 30s stepped in. Jeanemarie pressed herself up against him, wrapped her arms around his neck, and gave him a long passionate kiss.

"Well," I mused to my miserable self, "I guess she just likes expensive restaurants and Broadway plays."

"Losing" her only deepened an already deep sense of loneliness. I had stopped practicing my religion. I was working at night and on weekends. I was living in an apartment far above the earth. I was living a life so far removed from people my age that I had emotionally sealed myself away from people who could have helped. I kept up a cheerful front at work, but on the inside I ached badly.

I needed to get back to basics; to my link with God, and to the sense of optimism that I had known at Warm Springs.

I felt trapped, but I knew no way of getting out of the trap. Being under the tutelage of a cynical and burned-out case did not help.

Why had I been drawn to Metcalf, who went out of his way to goad people? Every night he would look across to the far side of the desk at Charlie "Sarge" Mulcahey, a kindly man in his late-50s. In a stage whisper around 11:30 Metcalf would say, "See, he just took his Valium, and is starting his countdown to bed."

Metcalf was a deep reader in the history and downfall of Nazism. His ex-wife, of whom he professed deep hatred, was Jewish. He enjoyed baiting Steve Esrati, a Jew from Cleveland Heights who had served in the Israeli army. With his back toward Esrati, Metcalf would say in that stage whisper, "You know, Martin Borman (one of Hitler's henchmen) is living in Shaker Heights and is working in a Jewish bakery." Shaker Heights historically had a large Jewish population.

Maybe I was too young and too stupid to understand how deeply Metcalf could wound people by his words. On the other hand, he was extraordinarily funny at times. One time he saw the ancient movie critic at the "Plain Dealer," Ward Marsh, taking a nap far back in the darkened "day" section. "Look," Metcalf said, "there's old Ward Marsh staring at the wall waiting for the movie to start."

He surprised me one night by offering me a ride home. He drove a Renault, very unusual for the '60s, and bragged of its Michelin tires. He got me into the car, and we roared down Superior Avenue, a six-lane street. He was screaming and cursing at other drivers. He became so incensed at the slower driver in front of him that he turned the car up onto the wide sidewalks next to St. John's Cathedral, careened around the corner and headed toward the lake.

Metcalf roared onto the West Shortway passing a line of cars waiting to get on the freeway on the up-ramp near old Cleveland Municipal Stadium. I thought I was in a cartoon movie where the driver sticks his head and arm outside the window screaming insults at other drivers while going 100 mph.

"Now I am really going to die here on this bridge two hundred feet above the mouth of the Cuyahoga River," I thought to myself. Then I began to laugh so hard that tears poured down my face.

We roared out to my apartment building where we entered the underground garage. We screeched to a halt in front of the entrance to the lobby of the second underground level. Metcalf had put the folded wheelchair in the trunk, which was in front. He had trouble getting it out, so he climbed up into the trunk cursing and preparing to do battle with the wheelchair.

Some people dressed in formal evening attire came along. The group stopped at the sight of this tall bony man jumping up and down in the front-end trunk cursing at a wheelchair.

Metcalf stopped, looked down at them and screamed, "Don't worry, folks, the kid's OK, he's just crippled!" They fled into the building.

Soon after that he got his medication adjusted. From that point onward he was still caustic and sarcastic, but no longer as volatile.

I once joked with my older brother Tom when I was a junior or senior in college that I was eating aspirin like candy. In fact, those headaches in college became real headbangers after I started my work life. It did not help matters that I was beginning to drink after work. Most of the people who gave me a ride home stopped first at the Headliner bar next to the newspaper.

At first, it was just beer. Soon it became a shot and a beer, then three or four of those potent combinations. In addition, everyone on the copy desk smoked. Some of them smoked everything in one night's shift: cigarettes, cigars, pipes. Some also chewed tobacco, and used the green metal wastebaskets for spittoons. One had to be careful in retrieving paper.

"Why fight it?" I asked myself. "If I'm going to work under this damn gray cloud over the copy desk, I may as well join in."

I began to bum cigarettes. Then I started buying my own in the vending machine next door in the cafeteria. At my apartment, I would smoke two or three a day. That was not a lot except for someone with a left lung that had been atrophied by polio. It was really only half a lung.

I could very well have set myself aflame. I was operating with only one moderately-strong hand, half a bicep, and no triceps. I would sit by the window and watch the teeny-tiny humans far below while I inhaled deeply, and got the slight buzz.

My apartment was so high in the sky that during the annual Cleveland Air Show, an Air Force jet flew by my window and I actually exchanged waves with the pilot. Outside my large window was a concave-shaped ledge. On the opposite sides it was about 24 inches deep. However, in the middle it dipped in to about 12 inches. The window washers were lowered in a metal basket held by ropes and winches. They would step onto the ledge with no safety harness and proceed to clean the window.

One misstep and they would die. I felt as if I was dying slowly of loneliness. I thought to myself, "This must be the true essence of hell: seamless, unending loneliness."

My days off were Tuesday and Wednesday. I often went forty-eight hours without talking to anyone, except the barber. I got a haircut every week. For a few minutes, I got human conversation for $5.

One night, I had eaten one of the early "TV dinners." In those pre-microwave days you had to peel away part of the tinfoil and then put the dinner into the oven. Then 20 minutes into the cooking process one had to re-cover the uncovered area. I ate my Swanson's fried chicken dinner and threw the empty platter into the garbage can.

I took my fork and my spoon over to the sink that was in the rounded corner of the kitchenette. I flipped the fork and spoon up into the sink. Then I unlocked my foot platforms and swung them back out of the way.

I slid forward in the wheelchair in order to be able to reach the handles for the hot and cold water. I pushed my knees tight up against the doors below the sink, and locked both brakes. I turned on the hot water full blast intending to moderate it with cold. Before I could do so, the spoon slid down into the drain.

Without thinking, I stuck my hand down the drain. It immediately became stuck in the drain. The scalding hot water was pouring down on it painfully. For once I did not think. I acted instinctively.

With all the strength I could muster, I lunged backward in the wheelchair and pulled with all my strength on the hand. It already was beginning to swell. It stuck for a sliver of a second, then popped free. From becoming stuck to being free took no more than five seconds. If I had stopped even a few more seconds to ponder the problem, it might have been a fatal delay.

It would have been a long, slow, painful clinging to consciousness before I would have blacked out. It would have been 48 hours until someone at work noticed that I was not there. There was no way to call for help. Rarely did I hear people moving in the hallway. When I did, the thick walls and the heavy door muffled the sounds.

I thought of a headline some of the smart-alecks on the desk might have suggested: "Young Copy Editor Dies in Lakewood as Life Goes Down the Drain." Trembling, I went over to the window and looked at all the lights far below. They reminded me of Christmas tree lights on the floor plugged in to find "dead" bulbs.

None of those lights held any warmth for me. After I stopped trembling, I typed a letter to my old department head, Jay Jensen, at Illinois asking if I could get into graduate school in communications and if he had any financial help available. I typed a memo seeking a leave of absence to one of the numerous assistant managing editors.

Jensen said he could get me into graduate school for the fall semester '67, and could offer me a partial assistantship. It would pay my tuition and give me $150 month. It was only June, but I was already mentally packing my bags.

I was lonely in my apartment. I was lonely in the crowd at work. For 14 straight months, I fought the shadowy ghosts of loneliness.

I was probably just too young to be in that environment. Maybe it was simply a case of biting off more than I could chew. I was suffering from sensory overload, and a sort of dehydration of the spirit. I desperately wanted a girlfriend, someone who would listen to my troubles, and offer some intimacy. Like most other normal young men, I thought of intercourse. But that was not what I was really seeking. I needed someone to say, "I love you, Jerry."

If that someone was in Cleveland, I had not found her.

On August 31, 1967, 14 months after I had begun work at the "Plain Dealer," I left Cleveland. When I moved into my new graduate student apartment, I found that I could not get up over the rise into the bathroom. So I called the Rehab Center. They sent their jack of all trades, Bob Fink, who built on the spot a long sloping entry into the bathroom. That night I got onto the commode on my elevated seat, and could not get off.

This time, the walls were not thick, nor was the unlocked door. An old friend from undergraduate days, a middle-aged man in a wheelchair, heard my calls for help and came over to drag me off.

After 14 months as a copy editor, it should have been clear to me that as long as I stayed in newspapers I would remain a copy editor—typecast, as it were. But I thought if I could substitute more education for reportorial experience, I might have a chance to become a columnist or an editorial writer.

Illinois offered a two-track choice in graduate communications. The first was a track ending with a master's degree in journalism. The second was a track leading to the doctorate in communications.

I chose the first. I think it was a choice born of fear. I feared letting go of the job that was still mine back in Cleveland. It gave me "standing" among the other graduate students and the professors. And I had a fear of failure at the higher levels of academia.

Gene Graham had taken a leave of absence. He was suffering from a cancerous brain tumor. I missed him very much, but another friend on the faculty, Charles Puffenbarger, took me under his wing. He had been a longtime reporter and editor at the "Washington Post." I graded the papers for his copy-editing class.

I graded them very harshly. "Puff" asked me to take over the class once when he was going to be away. When I rolled into the class, the students all booed.

Another acquaintance from undergraduate days in my dormitory showed up one night. He had heard that I was back in school. He came bearing a "gift:" an underground porno flick. He used the wall for a screen. It was an hour's worth of mindless coupling and sucking with enormous close-ups of a naked man and woman.

I felt as if I needed to wash my brain and heart.

I renewed a friendship with Lynn, who had been two years behind me in my undergraduate days. She walked with short leg braces and the kind of metal crutches that fit over the wrist. She had long blond hair. When it was not tied into a ponytail or piled on her head, it reached all the way down to the small of her back. She had a pink complexion. And she had very large breasts.

She began coming over to the apartment and cooking meals for me. We would sit on the couch together and neck. She took the fun out of it after several sessions by saying, "Ron Timpson (former Rehab student) kisses a lot better than you do."

One night, she suggested we lie down together on my narrow bed. "You go first," she said. Startled, I got into bed. She followed. Her head was lying on my useless left arm effectively pinning me to the bed. I could not roll toward her. She began crying and telling me of her recent breakup with "Bill."

"We have been going to Springfield and staying overnight and making love in a motel for months," she said between sobs. "I miss him so much, but he wants to get married right now and I said that we should wait."

"Oh, this is priceless," I said to myself. "I am finally in bed with a good-looking girl, and all she wants to do is cry about her 'Bill.'"

After several hours of memories of Bill and their love trysts, she got up and said, "Thank you very much. I feel much better. I think I will be able to patch things up with Bill. I needed to make him a little bit jealous." She called for a taxi. It arrived. I slammed the door shut. Then I slammed shut the book on Lynn.

After Jeannemarie had rolled over my heart back in Cleveland, I hurt badly for months. In Lynn's case, the hurt did not run deep. My ego had been bruised, and my bad luck with women was holding true.

Still, the nine-month timeout back in school was giving my emotional batteries a recharge. Spiritually, my laziness continued as I pushed to the back of my mind the simple fact that God offers no free passes. With God, the important thing is not how fast you can run, but how selflessly you can love.

I took a course in world communications taught by a Marxist. His contention was that Americans had an unconscious assumption of power. Our grade depended on one major paper due at the end of the course. Several weeks before that, we were to give a brief oral outline of our papers.

I came up with the cockamamie idea of going through two years' worth of Steve Canyon cartoons on microfilm with the idea of showing the "unconscious assumption of power."

I actually found a strip set in a remote village in the highlands of Vietnam. In one of the panels in the strip was a Coca-Cola sign hanging over the door of a small shop. When I gave my oral report during our weekly seminar session, I mentioned that panel.

"See! That is what I mean by American hubris and its unconscious sense of power! This man has touched the essence of this course!" the professor said. For one horrified moment, I thought a Marxist was going to kiss me. Fortunately, the bell rang.

My finest collegiate moment came in graduate school. I had taken an upper-level history course on the urbanization of America after the Civil War.

As a graduate student, I had to write a "historiographical essay" on the subject. That kind of essay surveys, analyzes, and critiques the historical writings on the subject. I checked out 27 books from the 10-story Illinois library and took them home at Christmas time. I spent the entire vacation at the family dining room table reading, taking notes, thinking, and typing.

The professor returned the paper with an "A+" on it.

His written comment was far more gratifying: "You have captured the essence of the soul of an historian." If there ever were a clarion call to change professions, that was it. I heard the call, but I did not answer.

I left my beloved university a second time. I had five years to write my master's thesis. My long-term plan now was to complete the master's degree and look for a teaching job in a college. So it was back to the lonely life in the high-rise apartment building, the nights on the "Plain Dealer" copy desk, and Metcalf on July 1, 1968.

End of Chapter 6

CHAPTER 7

"My Future Walked by . . ."

In the spring of 1968, I wrote to the assistant managing editor in charge of lost causes at the "Plain Dealer" to tell him that I wanted to return to work on July 1.

He wrote back saying that was fine with the "Plain Dealer," and added that they had hired two copy editors. One was Judd Shelnutt, who was coming from some small paper in western Pennsylvania. He lived in Geneva-on-the-Lake, about 45 miles east of Cleveland.

The other was Dave McLean, who was from the "Painesville Telegraph." Painesville is about 30 miles east along the lakeshore from downtown Cleveland. The assistant managing editor mentioned that McLean had one good eye. The other was glass.

"And Metcalf thought they were scraping the bottom of the barrel when they made me their first copy editor to come directly out of college, and the first person in a wheelchair to work in the newsroom," I said out loud to myself. "I can only imagine how he greeted the one-eyed guy." I suspected this kind of interaction:

Metcalf: "Hey, kid, which eye are you usin' tonight?"

McLean: "Don't worry, I'll get the job done."

Metcalf: "When you go for coffee, keep turning right (McLean's glass eye was his left)."

On that first day of July 1968, I got up at the usual time of noon which gave me more than 3 1/2 hours to wash up, take care of the toileting, and dress. Then I called a cab.

(Suburban taxi companies could take me into the city but could not pick me up in the city. Yellow Cab used the old Checkers cabs. Their seats were deeply recessed, making it impossible for me to get in by using my sliding board. So I depended upon fellow workers to get me home).

When Metcalf saw me coming toward the copy desk that first night back, he waited until I had almost reached my accustomed spot next to his on the far left corner of the desk. Then he stood and said in a stage voice, "First they hired a cripple, then they hired a guy with one eye. My God, here we are, the halt, the lame, and the blind."

"You want some coffee, kid?" he said. I was home again.

July, August, and most of September passed uneventfully, except for the banishing of me on Friday and Saturday nights to the sports department's copy-editing crew on prep football Fridays and college football Saturdays.

There was a midget who worked as a sportswriter in a sort of second-string role.

He was very annoying. He was constantly looking in wastebaskets around the newsroom, apparently seeking private information. One Friday night, he was scrounging through a wastebasket. Danny Coughlin, a talented Irish-American sports reporter, grabbed the little guy and dropped him into a three-foot-high industrial-strength wastebasket. The basket rocked back and forth while the midget screamed with a metallic echo, "Let me out! Let me out! I'll tell on all of you!"

Someone else pulled him from the basket and set him on a shelf on the wall six feet above the floor. Finally, cooler heads prevailed upon Coughlin and his fellow tormentor to get the little person down.

Occasionally I also was sent to the nearby national news desk when national editor Ted Mellow was on vacation. Mellow's demeanor matched his name. He was tall, extremely literate, and easygoing. His assistant, Walter Berkov, was the exact opposite in many ways. He was very talented, but he was nervous and hard to please. He would toss me a national news story, and say, "Rewrite this to about nine inches."

I would painstakingly rework the story and turn it over to Berkov. He would take his copy editing pencil and furiously strike through everything I had done. He would retype the entire thing. "Why do they bother sending me?" I would say to myself.

My first copy desk chief was a suave, debonair man named Bob Havel, who always was impeccably dressed in a tailored suit. Every night when he came to work in the middle of the U-shaped copy desk, he would carefully remove his suit coat, put it on a hanger, and hang it from one of the pipes running over the copy desk. He wore a silver bracelet, as well as an expensive-looking watch. He always wore expensive-looking ties and suits.

From the beginning, Havel treated me with dignity and respect. He was very patient with me, bringing me along very slowly. He often gave me a ride home. He also lived in Lakewood. However, before heading to Lakewood, we would stop with several other editor types at a bar several blocks from the "Plain Dealer."

It was there that Havel introduced me to the deceptively powerful martini. After I downed the first one in the way one would swig a glass of pop, Havel said, "Unless you want to be carried out of here instead of being rolled out, I would suggest that you sip the next one slowly. We will keep you at two per night for some time to come."

Havel had the impressive ability to drink at least ten cups of black coffee a night, and only go to the men's room once. One time "Sarge" Mulcahey said, "Bob, I don't know how you do it, drinking all that coffee and never seeming to be bothered enough to get up several times for a run to the head."

I piped up, "Charlie, haven't you ever noticed the hole in the floor next to Havel's right foot?" Havel did not seem to be amused. Soon after my return to the "Plain Dealer," Havel was promoted directly from the copy desk to a reporting position in the Washington bureau.

Coffee had a way of roaring right through me. So I often was forced to call upon one of the male copy persons (there were girls now) to take me to the men's room.

Many times that would be the chief of the copy person staff, Dennis Kucinich, who would later become the "boy mayor" of Cleveland, and who is now the popular congressmen from the west side of Cleveland. He has had a long ego trip as a candidate for the Democratic presidential nomination.

Kucinich quickly became known as "Dennis the Menace." He called himself an urban populist. He was, and is, a total opportunist, albeit a likable one.

On the cold drizzly night of Sept. 21, Marty Ranta, a friend from Lakewood, said, "My wife Virginia is coming down to take me home after work. She needed the car for church work. Would you like a ride home?"

An offer of a ride was like a small bit of manna from heaven, even if it was from a Jehovah's Witness. It meant that I did not have to beg someone for a ride. I immediately said yes.

After work, we were waiting in the lobby. Another copy editor, Carl Romansky, stepped out of the elevator and said, "Jerry, do you want a ride?" I hesitated and then said, "No thanks. Marty has offered me one." Ranta said, "Hey, my feelings won't be hurt if you go with Carl." I said to Romansky, "No thanks, Carl. I'll take a rain check."

Ranta's wife Virginia pulled up outside in an old Ford Fairlane station wagon. This was in 1968, and the federal government had only begun to require seatbelts on new cars in 1965, and then only two lap belts upfront. In older American cars built before 1965, there were no seatbelts.

Ranta helped me get into the front seat. Another editor, an Englishman by the name of Cedric Pulford climbed into the seat behind me.

Ranta's wife said, "Marty, maybe you ought to drive because of the rain." He said, "No, you'll do fine."

We crossed the Cuyahoga River on the Detroit-Superior Bridge, and veered slightly to the right to take the up-ramp onto the West Shoreway. We entered the freeway in the far left lane, the speed lane, and Virginia eased the car across three lanes to the slower outside lane.

Just as we passed the West 49th Street exit, Virginia cried out, "Marty, I can't control the car." The car was "hydroplaning," that is, virtually floating on the cold water on the freeway surface.

Marty reached up over his wife and grabbed the steering wheel to try to straighten out the car. It was of no use. We began to spin around and around. The spinning action probably increased our speed to over 60 mph. I said to myself, "I don't believe this is happening. I just don't believe this is happening."

Then my carefully planned world exploded. The noise was deafening as the car crashed into the metal divider on the freeway, bounced off, and crashed back into the divider, again and again as the car picked up speed going down a long straightaway. When we stopped several hundred yards down the road, the car was in the middle of the freeway pointed eastward.

I was lying up across the steering wheel with my head on the dashboard. I had never had a broken bone before in my life. But I knew immediately that there were breaks in my ankles, breaks in at least one knee and possibly the other. I knew that my lifeless left arm was cracked near the shoulder.

It was rather uncomfortable lying across the steering wheel with my face in a heap of glass shards, so I asked to be put back down on the seat. Marty and someone else did that. As they lowered me onto the seat, I felt a stabbing, ripping pain in my right hip and above that in my pelvic area.

Never had I hurt this bad, even in the darkest days of polio.

Several "Plain Dealer" people who were also on their way home stopped and helped to direct traffic so that we would not be hit by an oncoming car. It took the police only a few minutes to arrive.

Beyond the pain, my immediate concern was keeping Virginia calm. She had hurt her knee, and the trauma combined with pain from the knee had her on the edge of hysteria. "The last thing I need right now is someone going berserk on the seat beside me," I told myself.

"Virginia," I said, "things will be just fine as soon as they get us to a hospital. Just hold on a little while longer. Be strong, hold on."

When two policemen arrived with an ambulance in their wake, the officers hurriedly discussed where I should be taken.

"Where you think we should go—Lutheran Medical or St. John's?" one officer asked. We were midway between the two hospitals.

"Uh, well, let's take him to St. John's," the other said. On such decisions by strangers do lives turn. Four or five men had to rip off the twisted front door.

I asked them when I was on the gurney to leave my right knee bent upward. I thought that would lessen pain in one area, but as the ambulance began taking corners quickly, the broken bones on the right side seemed to grate together and sent waves of jagged pain washing over me.

I was soon on the emergency room table at St. John's Hospital. The emergency room nurse began undressing me. "I think there is at least one break in my left ankle. Just cut the shoe off," I said.

She said, "Oh, we don't want to ruin your nice loafers." With that, she yanked off the shoe. I cried out at the stabbing pain.

The emergency room doctor had been looking at the initial x-rays. He then began to pick out the bits of glass imbedded in my face and started to stitch up several deep cuts on my face. He asked the nurse, "Who is the orthopedic surgeon on call tonight?"

"Dr. Radkowski," she answered.

"Call him, and get him in as soon as possible," the ER doctor said.

It was the era of Polish jokes. I said to myself, "That's all I need now—a Polish bone surgeon." Apparently, the pain killer was kicking in.

The narcotic Demerol was given to me immediately after x-rays were taken. The pain from the eight or nine fractures receded as a blessed numbness spread over me. I was given Demerol on demand for at least a week.

Ranta's wife had badly bruised her knee. Ranta himself was uninjured. The other passenger, the Englishman Pulford, had a cut on his forehead. He refused stitches. My injuries were much more severe because there was no way I could put out my arms to protect myself, and in most areas of my body there was little muscle mass for padding.

Ranta waited until 6:30 a.m. to call my parents. My father had just gotten up for the day when the call came. It woke my mother, and she got up and sat on the edge of the bed. When he asked, "How bad are Jerry's injuries?" she let out a small gasp and said, "Oh, God, not again!"

The Demerol got me through the night. The pain would rush back in waves. Another shot of Demerol would bring the blessed numbness.

At my bedside early in the morning was a man who identified himself as Dr. Casimir Radkowski. He was wearing a blazing-red sports coat underneath his unbuttoned white hospital jacket. He told me of the broken bones—two in my left ankle, and possibly one in the right ankle; at least one in my left knee; another in my right knee; a broken left shoulder; a break, possibly two in the hip bone, and big cracks in the pelvis.

"You're going to need surgery on that right hip and pelvis," he said. "We will put a rod about seven inches long with a bend in it so that we can attach it to the pelvis. It will be there permanently. Also, we will not put casts on you so as to minimize loss of muscle strength. We are simply wrapping you in Ace bandages."

Then he said, "Your mother, father, and younger brother are waiting out in the hall to see you. I will be seeing you soon in surgery."

With that, he gave me a keep-your-chin-up pat in an area that was not broken, and went to get my family. With my face bruised as well as stitched, with the stitches plainly visible, and with the Ace bandages all over my body, I was not a pleasant sight.

When my father got to my bedside, he immediately turned around and left the room. Outside, he slumped to the floor. Dr. Radkowski saw him go down and rushed to help him. He then called the family together in the hall and explained what needed to be done.

My mother stayed at my apartment. She was at my bedside

daily for the short period of time they allowed relatives into Intensive Care.

I was moved to the Intensive Care Unit. I was unaware of it, but the concern was that tiny bits of bone or other flotsam and jetsam would break loose from the areas of the fractures and move to my heart. They wanted to keep a close eye on me by putting me in ICU.

The place was staffed with a large number of cute young Licensed Practical Nurses, or LPN's. They had little to do but to check dials and gauges.

Most of them spent time at my bedside just talking. I spent two weeks in the place, so after awhile I began to collect names, addresses, and phone numbers. I figured if I ever made it back to Cleveland and to my job, I would have a list to work from. On the morning of my second day in ICU, I was wheeled off to surgery. I awoke feeling a huge soft bandage on my right side in the area of the hip.

The day after surgery I awoke from a nap to see Dr. Radkowski and two of the young nurses at my bedside. "I want to check to see if your right knee is broken," Dr. Radkowski said. "We can usually tell by the color of the blood drawn from the area. I am sorry, but this is going to hurt."

He wasn't kidding. He took a large syringe with a large needle and inserted it into the knee joint. "Only marginally better than the car wreck itself," I told myself as he probed with the big needle. I was squirming and moaning. I saw a look on his face that said: "The patient is in extreme pain."

"I am very sorry for your discomfort," he said after withdrawing the needle. The syringe was filled with liquid the color of coal dust. "Is there a break there too?" I asked.

"Yes, definitely," he said. "We had better wrap this knee also."

After my time in ICU, I was out of danger. They moved me to a floor called "3-West." The nurses referred to it as "bones and stones." People recuperated there from fractured bones, and others who had gallbladder operations also recuperated there.

At first I was in a four-bed room. On my first night there, a very overworked and very pretty young nurse asked how she could make me comfortable. I said, "You have enough work as it is without taking the time to get all of my various parts adjusted." But she insisted on helping, and she made the time to do it.

The three other men in the room were a foul lot, and made it a very uncomfortable place. My mother asked that I be moved to a double-bed room. She was promised that as soon as one came open, I would be moved.

Another young LPN got me up into my wheelchair and wheeled me out into the hall, where I could at least see something different and possibly interesting. I certainly did see something different and interesting.

As I sat in the hallway, my future walked past.

A young nurse with a stunning figure and a smile so bright that its glow warmed me walked by. She had short-cut soft brown hair framing a face of pure joy. She smiled directly at me in a friendly, totally innocent manner. I watched her walk down the hallway, and saw the finest-shaped rear end I had ever seen on a girl.

Apparently, her head nurse decided to play Cupid. I was moved into a two-bed room. The other bed was empty. That nurse who had lit up my life for those few moments in the hallway was assigned to me. Her name was Mary Jean Koch. To her friends, she was "Jeannie."

In her first shift, I learned the depth of her young-womanly modesty. I rang the bell, and when she entered the room, I said, "I need to use the urinal." She came back with one, turned her head away, lifted up the sheet, and threw the urinal under the covers. She hurried out of the room. I had to ring again.

"Uh, excuse me, but I cannot use this without help," I said. "Oh, I'm sorry," she said with her face reddening from embarrassment. She managed to position my penis without looking, and then went across the room until I was done.

We began to talk as much as possible. After her first eight-hour shift of helping me, I had someone throw away that list of names, addresses, and telephone numbers gathered in ICU.

"This is the girl that I am going to marry," I said to myself at the end of that first day. Forget all the painful false starts, forget all the time spent worrying if I was ever going to find a girl who would say, "Jerry, I love you."

I had found her quite by accident.

For five days, we talked of each other's hopes and dreams. Hers were very simple and straightforward: "I want a guy who will love me, who will be faithful to me, who loves children and wants to have lots of them, and most of all who can share my love of God," she said.

"I want to have about 10 children," she said, "how about you?"

"That sounds good to me," I replied.

"All's fair in love and war," I told myself.

There was no doubt that love was exploding from two different directions and co-mingling in that hospital room over those five days. On the fifth day, I was told that I was being discharged the next morning. I gave Jeannie my parents' address and telephone number in Dover. She gave me her home phone and address. She was the 10th child of a family of 13. She and two younger siblings, a sister and brother, were still living with her parents on West 114th Street, just two blocks from the Lakewood border.

We were only one mile apart during my first 14 months in Cleveland.

The next morning I was placed on a gurney, and was about to be wheeled out of the room when the phone rang. It was Jeannie. "Please write to me, won't you, Jerry?"

She hesitated, and then said the words I had long hoped to hear: "I love you, Jerry Range."

"You bet that I will write you. I love you too, Jeannie Koch."

Then after those five days in which I had found the person I had been looking for, I dropped out of her sight for four months. Those four months only intensified my desire for her. At Christmas time, I sent her a crystal rosary, a lace mantilla (many Catholic women still wore something on their heads in church), and a Perry Como album (a sure winner with a traditional Catholic girl).

In late January, the nine fractures had healed well enough to allow me to be back in my apartment in Winton Place. The very first thing I did was to call Jeannie and ask her to have dinner with me at Pier W, the swanky restaurant connected to my high-rise apartment building.

In my electric wheelchair, I met her in the lobby. Her younger sister Florence, and her younger brother Jim had come with her. They left her in the lobby with me. I showed her the barbershop, beauty shop, party room, and indoor pool. After the brief tour, we went into Pier W using the residents' private entrance. She had a strawberry daiquiri without the alcohol. I had a martini, with the alcohol.

After dinner, we went up to my apartment. I was living then on the 19th floor. I had pre-positioned a chair near the window. "Jeannie," I said, "let's just sit and enjoy the view of downtown Cleveland." As she marveled at the sights, she leaned forward to see people far below. I slipped my arm around the back of the chair.

As she sat back, I cradled her in my right arm. This beautiful, soft, warm, generous-hearted girl looked up at me and I leaned down and softly but firmly kissed her. Her right hand rose and her fingertips gently touched my left cheek.

As I pulled away, she said, "Why Jerry Range, why Jerry Range . . ." We kissed again, and then she laid her head against my right shoulder with her forehead snuggled up against my cheek. We sat like that in soft warm communion watching the stars, the lights below, and listening to each other's breathing, and to our own two hearts beating the notes to the same gentle tune.

We began seeing each other as often as possible. Jeannie even changed her shift to 3 p.m. to 11 to come close to matching mine.

Then about a month later, her father, mother, younger sister and younger brother moved to Jacksonville, Fla., where one of her married brothers lived. I had guessed that her parents wanted her to come with them. She had told me that she was going to accompany them to Jacksonville to help them get settled.

I wrote her a letter: "If you want to stay with your parents in Jacksonville, I will understand," I wrote in part.

Moments after reading my sappy letter, she called and said, "You are not going to get rid of me that easy, Jerry Range. I love you, and I want to be with you. I will be back in two weeks, and in the meantime I will pray for you. I love you, Jerry."

She was indeed back in two weeks. She would not have had a place nearby to live, because her father had sold the family home. Her sister the sister, Sister Audrey Koch of the Sisters of St. Joseph, asked friends in the convent at St. Rose of Lima Church, Jeannie's home parish, if she could live with them. They welcomed her.

Our dating consisted mainly of dinners at Pier W, or dinners that Jeannie cooked in my kitchenette. On the nights I was working and she was not scheduled, she would wait until 1 a.m. and then call me.

One night during a soft and low telephone conversation, I heard the gentle sound of a young lady snoring. I quietly hung up the phone and waited. Forty-five minutes later, Jeannie called and said, "I'm sorry, I'm sorry, I'm sorry. Please forgive me."

"Forgive you for what? For being tired? I knew you would call back."

On our "off" days, Jeannie would stay at the apartment until three or four in the morning. We would talk some, kiss some, talk some, kiss some, and talk some more, and kiss some more.

One night she became very serious, and a single tear rolled down her cheek. "I am so afraid of something," she said. "I'm afraid that we will not be able to share God's love."

"Jeannie," I replied, "please be patient with me. It has been a number of years since I broke off communication with God, with his son Jesus, and the Blessed Virgin Mary. I will need time and your help to repair that line of communication."

"I love you, Jerry Range," she said.

"I know, and it feels great," I said.

On April 2, 1969, I asked her to sit at the end of my bed. She seemed puzzled by my serious-looking face. "Will you marry me, Jeannie?" I asked.

"Yes, yes, yes," she said.

"I don't have enough money now to get you a diamond ring, but if you can wait for a few months I will get one."

"I don't need a ring," she said. What she did not know was that my friend Marty Ranta knew a jeweler who belonged to his "Kingdom Hall," which is what Jehovah's Witnesses call their churches. That jeweler sold me a $900 ring for $400. A week after Jeannie agreed to marry me, she was at my apartment fixing dinner. I asked her to come out into the room.

"Someone left this here for you," I said, while fumbling in my shirt pocket. "Reach in this doggone pocket and get this thing."

"I don't want the hamburger to burn," she said. But she honored my request and pulled out of my shirt pocket her engagement ring.

Tears of joy are wondrous to see. She sat on my lap, wrapped her arms around my neck and kissed me. "What about the hamburger?" I asked.

"What hamburger?" she asked.

She loved the heated indoor pool, and I loved seeing her in a bathing suit. Usually once a week, we would go down to the pool. She usually would have the pool all to herself with me waiting by the edge and a bored lifeguard at the far end of the room.

She was not an accomplished swimmer, but she enjoyed being in the warm water. And I enjoyed very much looking down the front of her swimsuit as she stood near the edge in the four-foot section of the pool.

Obviously, there was ample opportunity for us to become un-virgins. She knew very little about the mechanics of sex, but she was now very curious. So much so in fact that I bought a book written for engaged couples by a famed psychologist. I read it out loud so that we both could become more open about the subject of sex, and more open to the idea of understanding each other's needs and wants when we began intercourse after marriage.

Jeannie loved me and trusted me so much that it would have been easy to take advantage of her. But something deep down inside said, "Wait. Don't hurt her. Wait."

On many occasions when she was pressed up against me, my release valve opened. Jeannie never really knew the significance of my "aahs" at those times.

We scheduled our wedding for Sept. 27. I was so sure—100 percent sure—that this was the girl that I had been seeking, that in June I bought a new 1969 Rambler American, and handed it over to her for her own use. She kept the car at the convent, and drove it to work. She told me sheepishly that all the girls at work were jealous.

She did my grocery shopping for me, and we used the car for "real" dates like going to the movies, or just going for drives. I was beginning to get some Saturday nights off, and many Catholic churches in the Cleveland diocese were offering Saturday night masses. We began to attend churches all over the western suburbs.

We particularly liked St. Raphael's in Bay Village. It was there, however, that I first experienced what I would later know as symptoms of panic attacks. Often when we were in the church the walls would seem to expand outward and my heart would race.

Her father and mother flew back to Cleveland for the rehearsal dinner and wedding. Her mother was only then beginning that long dark march into oblivion called Alzheimer's Disease. Pier W had a small banquet room, and I reserved it for the rehearsal dinner. We were served champagne and prime rib.

I got a bit woozy, and my father had to take me outside for some air.

"Are you nervous?" he asked.

"No," I lied, "it's just the champagne on an empty stomach."

The wedding mass was set for 2 p.m. on Sept. 27. The day began rainy and gray. My younger brother Jim stayed with me overnight on the 26th. Bill Krantz, an old high school friend for whom I had been best man, returned the favor. Jim was my No. 2 guy at the wedding.

When Jim, Bill, and I went down to the lobby, it was raining hard. Bill went to get his car. Jim and I were outside under the canopy. An elderly woman came out and said, "You are going to be in the way when my husband drives over to get me."

"Lady," Jim said, "give the guy a break for God's sake, he's getting married!" She just mumbled about being inconvenienced, and was still mumbling as we drove away toward the church.

Jeannie set the tone for the rest of our marriage by being about 10 minutes late as the nuns, doing their version of the penultimate scene in "The Sound of Music," fussed over her in the back of the huge church with its magnificent stained-glass windows and its stunning sunburst design framing the mosaic crucifix behind the altar.

Jeannie came down the aisle on her father's arm with diamond drops glistening in her eyes. They say that every baby is cute, and every bride is beautiful. In Jeannie's case, the latter was not a cliche. Her father, a veteran of this sort of thing, gave her a goodbye kiss. She stepped toward me and gave me her hand. Bill rolled me around to her left, and she knelt beside me. I was 25, and she was 23. It was time.

I had rolled a very long way—90 miles from Erie, Pa., and a million miles back from the edge of the human scrap heap—to reach this spot in St. Rose of Lima Church.

On the way to the reception in the party room at Winton Place, the sun broke through the clouds, and blue sky was all about us. God was signaling A-okay.

I had never before seen my father cry. At the reception, he came up to me and with tears trickling down his cheeks said, "This is the happiest day of my life, Jer."

Jeannie went upstairs to "our" apartment to change clothes. Immediately after, I did the same. We drove away from the reception, but only got as far as the edge of the West Shoreway. I said, "Why bother going to a motel when we have an apartment in the sky?" So we returned to Winton Place, and as we were getting out of the car Jeannie's brother-in-law pretended not to see us.

We took the service elevator to the 19th floor. On the way up, my good right hand inexplicably found its way up underneath her green velvet dress. "Jerry, stop that until we get to the apartment! What if the elevator stops and someone gets on and sees you doing that? Now be good for a little longer."

In the apartment, with the door solidly locked, I asked my bride to undress. She did so with trust and without hesitation. Then with a girlish giggle, she jumped into bed and pulled up the covers. She threw back part of the covers invitingly. Using my sliding board, I got into bed. She gave me her virginity, and I gave her mine. Our marriage was thoroughly, totally, and repeatedly consummated on into the glorious bright night. I could not tell where my body ended, and where hers began.

There was only one Jeannie, and God had saved her for me.

End of Chapter 7

CHAPTER 8

"Babies, Back Stabbings, and Dayton"

There was an actual honeymoon beyond the apartment, in two parts. First, I took Jeannie up to Erie to show her where I had grown up. We stopped in front of my old house at 301 Gridley Ave. Then we drove down the block to pay my respects to old friends of my parents.

Their name was King. Mrs. King said, "You know of course who is living in your old house?" I said I had no idea.

"It is your old Little League coach, Joe Shugart. Why don't you go down and say hello." Jeannie went up to the front door, rang the bell and out stepped my old coach wearing a sweatshirt and, of course, a baseball cap.

He invited us in, and pulled me in my wheelchair up the front steps. When we got into the living room, he said, "Can I get you anything to drink? I'm having bourbon."

"Sounds good to me," I said. So my old Little League coach handed me a glass of bourbon and I sat sipping an alcoholic drink in my old living room. He called to his wife, who had her hair up in curlers. He also called to his 14-year-old daughter and his 11-year-old son. Both of them were in pajamas. No doubt the 14-year-old daughter was mortified, and the wife was probably doing a slow burn.

After a short time, we excused ourselves, and Shugart took me back down the steps. We drove away as my old Little League coach stood in front of my old house, waving goodbye.

A week later we flew out to Champaign-Urbana for homecoming. Illinois was playing Purdue. We were sitting in the midst of handicapped students, other alumni, and relatives.

As Purdue's quarterback turned to hand off the ball, it seemed to me that the fullback, who was to receive it, was limping. I yelled, "Get him, he's crippled!" There was stunned silence all around us. Jeannie giggled repeatedly that night at the motel at the recollection of my stupidity.

There was one sour note for her at the football game. She had to stand up and step aside so that an able-bodied young man could get to the main aisle leading out of the "horseshoe end" of the stadium where we were seated. The young man had to make a bit of an awkward climb to get around me and said to his friend in the aisle, "I hate cripples."

Jeannie looked straight at him, as she told me later, saying, "I wanted to ask him if he wanted to trade places with you. But I held my tongue."

"Welcome to my world," I said.

When we flew back to Cleveland, the airplane banked right over brightly lit Cleveland Stadium, where the Browns were playing a night game. It seemed as if Cleveland were saying to us, "Here I am. Take me."

Sex with my bride Jeannie was as good as I had always hoped sex would be. Whether it was in bed at night, in bed in the morning, on the couch before going to work in the afternoon, or in the dressing area or bathroom, it was an absolute gift.

Judging by the smiles on her face, and the singing that she did throughout the day, it seemed to be good for her also.

In fact, the sex between us was so good that five months after we married, Jeannie said she was pregnant. My reaction was, "Well, that's what sex does. It makes babies."

Other than her declaration in the hospital soon after we met that she wanted 10 children, we never really had discussed children. The assumption was if they come, they come.

She pleased me even more when she told me that her obstetrician said that sex could continue as long she felt comfortable. For us, that was all the way through the eighth month of pregnancy.

"What an incredible young woman I have married," I said to her. She seemed too good to be true. She still does. She continued to take me to work and to pick me up most nights after work at 12:30 a.m.

In fact, she picked me up at 12:30 a.m. on the night of Nov. 17, 1970, and delivered our first child six hours later. I was told to time the contractions, and not to worry about getting to the hospital until they were five minutes apart. So throughout the night in our apartment, I counted until we were down to five minutes. Then I called her brother-in-law, Leonard Strimpel, to take us to the hospital.

Michelle, or "Mickie" as she prefers to be called, was born 45 minutes after we got to St. John's Hospital.

Mickie was a wondrous thing to a young father.

When I came home from work, I would lie on our roll-out sofa bed and Jeannie would place little blond Mickie on my chest. As she lay there in her infancy, we would have deep philosophical discussions about the colors of the walls, about noises, about shapes and shadows, and about how lucky she was to have a mother named Jeannie.

Copy editor Judd Shelnutt asked me one night if Jeannie would be bringing me to work the next day. I answered yes. "Do you think you could have her come up to the copy desk?" he asked. Jeannie was very nervous about that kind of appearance, but I got her to agree.

When we went upstairs to the second floor of the "Plain Dealer" building, sitting near my workstation was a beautiful old-fashioned wooden rocker that obviously had cost Judd a fair amount of money. He said, "My wife and I would be very happy if you accepted this to use to rock your baby." Jeannie was overcome, and tearfully accepted. Thirty-four years later, she still uses that rocker.

Soon after Mickie was born, we moved to Apt. 804 in Winton Place. We actually had a bedroom of our own, plus a full kitchen, a large bath, and a very large living room. Mickie was installed in one corner of the living room. We put our kitchen table in front of the large picture window in the living room. We were on the back side of the building looking west. It was not as spectacular a view as 1911, but we still had the lake to watch. More importantly, we had some living space.

Jerry Jr. arrived in August 1972, making things a bit cozier in our apartment. He was colicky, and for about three months slept no more than three hours at a stretch. Jeannie's hands were strangely numb. I took her to the orthopedic surgeon who had put me back together. When Dr. Radkowski looked at her hands, and asked her a few questions, he said, "You have carpal tunnel syndrome."

He gave her medication, and soon her hands were back to normal. Again, the "Polish Falcon," as I called him, had done me a great service.

My work life was improving a bit. The closer a copy editor got to page one stories, the more his star was in the ascendancy. I was finally getting some page one stories to handle. The managing editor, a rotund Italian fellow named Ted Princiotto had been city editor. He was simply not cut out to be a judge of news outside Cleveland. But Tom Vail, the publisher, liked him, so that was that. The few times that I handled the top story, I would have to show the headline to Princiotto. It would take me about ten minutes to roll to his desk.

"Why doesn't the guy simply walk over to where I work?" I wondered.

The night that American astronaut Neil Armstrong stepped onto the moon, the 96-point headline (that is huge; a 72-point headline is one inch high) was ungrammatical. Several people argued with Princiotto, but the "Gondoleer," as he was derisively known on the copy desk, would not budge from what he had written himself. So the "Plain Dealer" the next morning had this odd headline: "MAN WALKS MOON."

Sometime in 1968 or early 1969, the "Plain Dealer" hired a copy editor named Artie. He had not gone to college. He had been the sports editor of a rural Ohio daily. After that, he had worked for a number of years at small papers in Michigan. Finally, after about 20 years in the business, the "Plain Dealer" gave him his big break.

From the very beginning, he began to sit on the inside of the desk across from Metcalf and me. When Metcalf was off, Artie would occupy his position. He would tell me grubby little stories of his sexual conquests. In intimate detail, he told me how he had deflowered a virgin while he was sports editor in that rural Ohio daily. It was something I really did not want to hear, but I was a captive audience. Seeing my discomfiture seemed to spur him on to more lurid details.

To my amazement, he was named the copy desk chief about the time of the birth of our first child. I had a bad feeling about the guy. For one thing, he played favorites, seemingly for his own amusement. We hired a copy editor from the old Columbus "Citizen-Journal." For about six months, the copy editor was Artie's fair-haired boy. He got top-of-the-fold page one stories to handle every night.

Then suddenly, he was handling nothing more than business shorts—little two—or three-paragraph stories that ran in the business section. The man was distraught. One night in the cafeteria, this 6-foot, maybe 230-pound man, sat with me at dinner. He asked me what he had done to fall into disfavor. I could give him no answer. Suddenly, this grown man sitting across the cafeteria table from me broke down in heavy sobbing.

My biggest gaffe came during the 1972 presidential campaign between Republican Richard Nixon and Democrat Sen. George McGovern. Nixon's wife Pat had made a speech for her husband in Cleveland. After the speech, one of our reporters asked her how her husband was faring physically on the campaign trail. She replied, "Well, he does get a bit tense on the campaign trail."

I wrote this headline on the story: "Dick tense on heavy schedule, Pat says." When the first edition came down, laughter began to erupt all around the desk. "What's so funny?" I asked someone. "Read what some nitwit wrote on the Pat Nixon story," the copy editor said.

My headline very quickly found its way to the main bulletin

board in the center of the newsroom. Soon, laughter was ringing out all around the place. You win some, and you lose some.

We had a young copy clerk by the name of Jimmy Ruffin. Jimmy was often assigned to the copy desk. He was not scared off by any of Metcalf's antics such as staring at the copy clerk and suddenly throwing a huge chunk of copy paper into the air, or walking down the copy desk to deposit his edited story in the wire basket near the copy desk chief, also referred to as "slot man."

Jimmy and I often talked. He was a reserved, well-mannered young man whose goal was to attend Cedarville College, not far from Dayton. Cedarville College was a fundamentalist Baptist school that required from its applicants a statement of how they had been saved by Jesus Christ.

Jimmy intended to become a minister, and return to his native Cleveland to establish his ministry in the black ghetto from where he came.

One night, about 7:30, he told me he was going out to McDonald's to get a burger. Four hours passed, and suddenly we all realized that Jimmy had not returned. The police beat was contacted, but our reporters had no information on him. About 11:30, he quietly slipped into his seat across from me behind the pneumatic tube.

"Jim, where have you been?" I asked. Others gathered around to listen. "I was at McDonald's sitting in my Volkswagen when a man with a gun got into the car, stuck the gun in my ear and said, 'Drive.'"

Jimmy drove for several hours around the east side of Cleveland. Finally, the man ordered him to stop in an alley. "I began to say my prayers so that God would welcome me into Paradise," he said. The gunman took Jimmy's wallet, pointed the gun at him, then inexplicably got out and ran off. Jimmy drove back to the "Plain Dealer" and quietly went back to work.

It wasn't as cataclysmic as Jimmy Ruffin's dance with death, but something that had been a part of my work life since I had come to the "Plain Dealer" died soon after Jimmy's harrowing tale.

Copy editors at the Plain Dealer worked roughly from 5 p.m. to about 12:30 a.m., depending upon when second-edition "proofs"—a copy of the main pages—were brought down from the composing room by the make-up editor, and cut up so that all of us got a chunk to read. Then we would go home.

One man worked 7:30 p.m. to roughly 3:30 a.m., at which time the paper was "put to bed," that is, there was no more chance to insert any more news. Dave McLean was the only person who wanted that god-awful shift. McLean, the one-eyed, ambitious young man out of Kent State University, wanted that shift to show the editors his ability to judge breaking news.

McLean thus got a few chances a each week to remake some of the pages for insertion of stories considered important enough or timely enough (a fatal shooting, for example) to remake the paper. I do not recall how his off-days were covered; one might have been on Saturday night when his shift was negated by the need to get out the huge Sunday paper which was started early on the presses. I do not recall how his other night off was covered.

In the summer of his second calendar year, McLean was eligible for two weeks of vacation. He probably would have reported for work had not his practical-minded first wife, Linda, made him stay away.

I found my name typed into the late shift for two weeks.

At that time, Michelle was nearing two years old. Jeannie was four months pregnant with Jerry Jr. She picked me up in our little white Rambler American on the first night with Mickie strapped into her car seat in the back. Downtown Cleveland at night in the early 1970s always was a scary place. At 3:30 a.m., it was a free-fire zone.

We drove down Superior Avenue to E. 9th Street, turned toward the lake, then turned left on Lakeside Avenue past City Hall. It was a mistake on my part.

Unfortunately, Lakeside Avenue passed a city park with fountains. In the daytime in good weather, city workers took their brown-bag lunches there. At 3:30 a.m., it was, as we learned to our horror, THE place to be for seemingly every ghoulish person in Cleveland. They filled the fountain area. They sauntered around in the street knocking on car windows looking for targets of opportunity.

The car in front of us stopped as the driver and walker, both men, fondled one another. There were freaks everywhere, a parade of gaudy human lizards. One walked up to Jean's door and tried to yank it open. Failing that, he started to batter on the window.

I yelled, "Gun the motor. I don't care who or what you hit!" Jean did and roared through the freak show leaving the ghouls screaming at us.

We both were scared out of our wits. When we reached home, I vowed I would get off the late shift. The next night I went to Artie and told him of the previous night's trouble.

He spit tobacco juice into his wastebasket and said, "Your name's on that shift on the goddam schedule and that's where it's gonna stay." I told him I would do anything else, but I had to get off that shift. He said, "Get the fuck out of my way, and stop whining."

The next night I tried again. His reply: "I told you last night you were on that shift for two weeks, now shut up!"

I wheeled over to the news editor, a mild-mannered fellow named Vern Havener. He had the power to override Artie's scheduling. I explained the situation to Havener, who said he would change the schedule if I put the request in writing. Then he withdrew his ever-present pipe from his mouth, leaned back in his chair and said, "You know what's going to happen, don't you?" alluding to retribution from Artie. "Yeah, I know, Vern, but Jeannie is scared and pregnant and I've got to get off that shift."

"OK," Havener said. He walked over to the schedule posted in the middle of the city room. I had given him a typed memo in which I spoke of "family responsibilities" in asking to be relieved of the shift.

Seeing Havener override him, Artie scribbled in Metcalf's name for the two-week stint on the late-late shift. Metcalf, who was second in seniority on the desk, was furious at me.

When I reported the next night at my customary position

next to Metcalf—my berth for six years—I found what it was like being caught in no-man's land between the trenches as both sides lobbed shells at me.

Artie bellowed, "HEY, JOHN, I CAN'T WORK TONIGHT BECAUSE OF FAMILY RESPONSIBILITIES!" Right on cue, Metcalf yelled back, "YEAH, I GOT FAMILY RESPONSIBILITES, TOO, ARTIE, BUT I GOT TO WORK THE LATE SHIFT!"

Metcalf was divorced, his two children were in their twenties, and he lived alone. But one man, Artie, had seen his authority overriden and another man, Metcalf, had been inconvenienced, and the sacrosanct seniority rule had been breached.

They kept up a constant drumfire of sarcasm for three weeks as the rest of the copy desk staff watched and listened. The pair was unrelenting in the vicious attack. Going to work became a heart-pounding exercise in apprehension and fear. Every man has his breaking point. I had finally reached mine.

I slammed the heavy paste pot down on the desk and turned to Metcalf and yelled into his face, "This what I get for six years of friendship, you fucking son of a bitch! This what Jeannie and I get for helping you, for taking you home from the hospital after surgery, and for buying you groceries and getting your medicines!"

I called out to a copy editor who had previously asked me to exchange lockers if he still wanted to do it. He did. A copy clerk emptied my locker and moved the contents to the other man's locker on the far side of the huge U-shaped desk.

The entire newsroom of some 150 reporters and editors was eerily silent. There is nothing so entertaining as listening to the breakup of a friendship. It is like watching two men slashing one another with razor-sharp knives.

"Thanks for nothing, you back-stabbing bastard, and that goes for your chicken-shit friend, our so-called slot man, Artie! With so-called friends like you two, I would never need enemies," I yelled. I laboriously rolled to the far side of the desk.

When I got to the other side, friendly "Sarge" Mulcahey said, "Welcome to the good guys' side, Jerry. We've been waiting for you. Glad to have you."

The constant barrage of sarcasm, barbed comments, and just plain viciousness ended immediately. Righteous anger is useful as a way to clear the air and to stake out your psychic territory.

For more than three months, I did not exchange one word with Metcalf. In late September, he came past my new location and said, "How ya doin', kid?" That was his way of burying the hatchet. As far as I was concerned, the hatchet was a permanent fixture in my back. I did manage to mumble, "OK, John. How you doin'?"

From then on until my career at the "Plain Dealer" ended, Metcalf and I would speak infrequently and very tersely. A friendship I had enjoyed, which had introduced me to a unique kind of man, was dead.

Of course, Artie gave me nothing more to handle than business shorts. He simply wanted me gone. I suspect he resented my college education, something he had never gotten. He saw my education as a shortcut to the kind of money and status for which he had labored at small papers for two decades.

He had worked in small backwater daily newspapers for 20 some years at poor wages and at probably much poorer working conditions before getting his big break at the "Plain Dealer." Then I showed up at age 22 with no experience and only my college degree.

Worst of all, I was a cripple.

Although my starting salary was below his journeyman's wage, I caught up to him after five years, because of the structure of the union contract. Ultimately, "Artie" got his revenge. And I handed him the fatal knife.

Jean and I had visited her brother Joe and sister-in-law Mary Beth in Jacksonville, Fla. I went down to the "Jacksonville Journal" and talked to the managing editor. In early December, he called and offered me a job at $250 a week. At that time, I was making $387 a week in Cleveland.

The adage in the newspaper business was that in the South, "They pay you in sunshine." I leapt before I thought it through. I accepted on the spot, wrote a letter of resignation with the customary two-week notice. After just one day, I began to count dollars. Common sense returned. I called Jacksonville and backed out of the offer.

At the time, the executive editor of the Plain Dealer was an expatriate Scotsman, Tom Guthrie. He had a reputation as being cheap. I submitted a note to Guthrie requesting that he rescind my resignation. I assumed it was a pro forma situation.

On the third night of the two-week notice period, his secretary came out to me and said, "Mr. Guthrie would like to see you."

Guthrie said, "I have your request to rescind your resignation, but, you know, once these wheels start in motion, it's hard to turn them around. You ought to work for a paper like the Elyria "Chronicle-Telegram" (a small daily in neighboring Lorain County). You would fit in at a place like that." What he was saying was that he and probably others in management regarded with distaste having a cripple in a wheelchair in the newsroom. I should have seen it coming.

Thus, my newspaper career in Cleveland ended. Obviously, Artie, who had a long memory, played a part in the decision not to rescind my resignation. It would have been standard policy for Guthrie to ask the opinion of the copy desk chief on such a personnel matter. Artie had gotten a chance at revenge.

The "Plain Dealer" did not get off Scot-free. The union officers of Local No. 1 of the International Newspaper Guild went to bat for me. They got me $3,400 in severance pay as well as a listing on the "Plain Dealer's" records that indicated I had left of my own volition. It took him a year and a half, but Artie got his revenge. Still it came at a significant cost in 1972 dollars to the "Plain Dealer."

Artie's career never progressed much. I often wonder if the $3,400 bite put on the "Plain Dealer" was a black mark in his dossier. For me, it was just another odd chapter in my "abnormal" life.

On my final day at work, Dec. 15, 1972, it had begun to snow early in the afternoon. Mickie was running a low-grade fever. A doctor called in a prescription to a pharmacy about ten blocks from us. It was rush hour, it was snowing heavily, and it took us about a half-hour to get to the pharmacy. While Jeannie was in the pharmacy, I said to myself, "This is ridiculous. The 'Plain Dealer' does not want me, my kid is sick, and I'm not going to make my young wife drive to downtown Cleveland in the snow."

So when Jean came out to the car, I told her to go home. A few minutes after we got into the apartment, the phone rang. It was the city room secretary. "Mr. Burdoch (the managing editor) wants to know when you will make it to work," she said.

"Tell Mr. Burdoch that I'm not coming to work," I said, "because No. 1, the 'Plain Dealer' has made it clear that I'm expendable, and No. 2, I'm not forcing my wife to drive downtown in a snowstorm."

Shortly thereafter, the phone rang again. The same young woman said, "Mr. Burdoch says he will send a taxi for you."

"Tell Mr. Burdoch," I said, "he and the 'Plain Dealer' can take that taxi and shove it up their tailpipes."

"Mr. Burdoch will not be happy about that," the dutiful young woman said. "That's fine," I said, "that's just fine with me."

Now I had no job. I had a beautiful young wife, a gorgeous little 2-year-old daughter, and an infant son. For the first time in many years, I felt the acidic taste of panic.

Letters and resumes sent to other wheelchair-accessible newspapers in northern Ohio went unanswered.

With great distaste, I called my former news editor in Cleveland, now an assistant managing editor at the "Dayton Daily News." He turned me over to the news editor, a gregarious-sounding fellow named Carl Beyer.

"We are looking for a new copy desk chief," Beyer said. I told him, "I don't want the power to schedule people's lives, and run a copy desk."

"Well," Beyer said, "come on down anyway, and have a look at us. We can go out to lunch and get acquainted." I accepted, and we set the date just before Christmas. My father and I went down to Dayton.

For lunch, Beyer took us to a restaurant regarded as the best in southwest Ohio, the King Cole. I had a great veal cutlet. Beyer was a likable sort of man, the kind of person you sensed wanted to be liked.

Back at the newsroom after the lunch, I chatted with Beyer and the assistant managing editor. They told me that they were looking for a copy desk chief who could help them get through the coming installation of computerized editing terminals, or VDT's (video display terminals).

I said, "I know a young guy in Cleveland who is very ambitious to move up, and who is energetic and enthusiastic. His name is Dave McLean. He sounds like the guy you are looking for." Beyer said, "Thanks for that information. We just might check into him. And you keep in touch. You never know when an opening will pop up."

They talked to McLean, and he accepted the job as copy desk chief in Dayton. Shortly after Christmas, I got a call from Beyer. "Would you like to be a copy editor in Dayton?" he asked. I told him that I had been making $387 a week in Cleveland. "Well, that's no trouble, we can hire you in at $50 over scale, which will put you at, well let's say an even $440 a week. That means as the salary scale increases overall, you will stay $50 above the journeyman level."

I was blown away by the offer. This time I asked if I could talk to my wife about it. "Sure," he said, "call me tomorrow." Jeannie was delighted. "Brother Ed (her elderly cousin, now deceased) is a member of the Society of Mary which owns the University of Dayton. And my uncle Jimmy is at the Veterans hospital in Dayton."

That sealed the deal. She was happy, and that made me happy.

I called Beyer the next day, and said, "You are going to have one happy copy editor." Again, I had leaped before I had looked.

End of Chapter 8

Easter Sunday, 1950.

Third-grade heartbreaker,
Jefferson School, 1953.

"Bring it on"—spring, 1955.

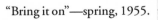

Graduation at Illinois,
June 1966.

Jeannie, LPN graduation,
August 1968, Lakewood, Ohio
Hospital School of Practical
Nursing.

Sept. 27, 1969: the brand-new Mr. and Mrs. Jerry A. Range.

At the "Jake" (Jacobs Field, Cleveland): my sons and I in the "front row" of bleachers; L-R: Jerry Jr., 31; Peter, 22; Christopher, 27; Patrick, 20; Dad, 59.

The gang's all here (L-R): Mickie, 33; Peter; Mary Rose (Range) Smolak, 29; favorite son-in-law Dr. Michael J. Smolak, 31; favorite daughter-in-law Karen (Paul) Range, 35; Patrick; Christopher; Jerry Jr., Karen's husband.

CHAPTER 9

"-25 Below, but I Still Can't Go"

I began work as a copy editor at the "Dayton Daily News" on Monday, Jan. 15, 1973. I was devastated emotionally by the first day at work. I wish it had been otherwise.

Unlike the "Plain Dealer," there was no pecking order among the copy editors in the editing staff.

There was no pecking order, because there was far too much work for the number of copy editors available.

There was no room for prima donnas, and no time for playing favorites. Withholding work from a copy editor to punish him would have punished everyone else on the rim. There was simply a mountain of work each day, and as soon as you finished one story, you grabbed another off the small mountain and began to edit.

The "copy desk" was basically six or seven old metal desks backed up against each other. The news editor and the assistant news editor would "dummy," or design, the pages, and throw the stories into wire baskets. Then the copy editors would take over.

On my first morning, the editing staff was leaner than usual. There were four of us. I did not move from the desk until about 10:45. I had been editing copy furiously since 6 a.m. I used a manual wheelchair that could be wheeled with one hand. It had two rims on the right side. I would grab the two rims in my "good" right hand. By pushing on both at the same time, I could go forward.

However, the men's room was far from the copy desk. So I

began to ask early on for assistance. It was embarrassing, but a puddle of urine on the floor would have been far more embarrassing.

The pace of work was frenetic. We started at 6 a.m., and finished about 2:30 p.m. The first deadline came at 10 a.m. At that time, the copy editors took about a 15-minute break. The next edition's deadline was 11:30, and the final edition deadline was 12:30.

On any given day, there was supposed to be five or six "rim men." Those were copy editors like me who trimmed news stories, wrote headlines on them, and wrote "art" lines (picture captions). On Saturdays, we split the copy-editing staff. I worked at night on the Sunday morning edition. Often there would only be copy desk chief Dave McLean, my old friend from Cleveland, and me.

I believe that McLean had worked behind the scenes to get me a job by making my hiring a condition of his taking the job as copy desk chief/newsroom computer guru.

My father and older brother Tom, who had just been discharged from the submarine service, had taken me down to Dayton in late December to find a place to live. We went to the "Daily News" building and talked with Beyer.

Tom cut right to the chase: "Tell me where most of the blacks live, and which direction they are heading." I confess I did not object. Beyer took us back to the wall map of the Dayton area in the photographic studio. He showed us that the black population was concentrated west of downtown, and that middle-class blacks were heading west into Jefferson Twp., and northwestward into the suburb of Trotwood.

Others had told me to go to Kettering, a suburb of 60,000 people in the hills south of the city. That's where we went.

Dayton was not a big city, but neither was it small. It had large indoor malls, and a mass transit system (it still included trolleys) to supplement its network of freeways.

Downtown Dayton was at the bottom of a bowl formed by the confluence of the Miami River and the Mad River. The two rivers became the Great Miami River. During the day, downtown Dayton throbbed with life. At night, it was a ghost town.

I opened a bank account, and the person helping us suggested we look at Georgetown Apartments in the suburb of Kettering.

For $235 a month, I rented lots of living space. There was parquet wood flooring, a spacious kitchen, a large living room, three bedrooms, and two baths backed up against each other in an L-shaped arrangement. There was also a small patio completely enclosed by a six-foot high wooden fence.

On Jan. 11, 1973, Jeannie and I drove down to Dayton with the kids. When she saw the apartment, she was ecstatic. It was flooded with light, giving it an airy feeling. It gave Michelle, who was 2, plenty of space to play. Jerry Jr. was then only five months old.

I very badly wanted things to work out for Jeannie's sake. Although her elderly cousin, Brother Ed of the Marianists, was at the University of Dayton, and her uncle Jimmy was in the Veterans Administration Hospital, the only person remotely near our age was another cousin. His name was Gene Votruba, a middle-aged man who lived with his wife in the suburb of West Carrollton, some 15 miles distant.

Essentially, we were on our own.

At times in my early days at the "Daily News," I thought we might just as well have been on an assembly line making "hemulators for Wuppermens," a mythical product that was the brainchild of sagacious copy editor Bob Brimm, who befriended me and gave me enormous emotional support.

An editor had to paste each page under the bottom of the previous page. Often it was necessary to cut sections out of one page and graft them into another page.

I was unable to use a scissors, so I developed a method of using a large slug of lead which one of the printers gave me. I would lay the long bar of lead across a page, and tear out a section. Then I would take the page where it was to be inserted, and repeat the process using white paste that newspapers in the pre-computer age had in enormous supply.

Some of the other editors would simply re-type an entire story, but with my weak wrist and lacking the kind of leverage that I would have had at home, I could not retype. I became adept and speedy at slamming down the bar of lead, ripping, slamming down the bar again, ripping, slamming down the bar on another page, ripping, slamming again, ripping, and finally pasting.

We finished on Saturdays at midnight. It was two or three in the morning before I could decompress from work and get to sleep. It would be late Sunday morning before I awoke. Jeannie would have to help me to get out of bed so that we could get to mass at noon. Never had I known such fatigue, both emotionally and physically.

The method of getting in or out of bed was the same that I had used back in my college days. Part of a long board that had been sloped at each end and on the front side would be inserted under my rump as I raised myself off the seat of the wheelchair by hooking my shoulder blades over the back panel. The other end would be on the bed.

I had enough strength in my right arm (there I had an opposable thumb, a weak wrist but a strong forearm and half a bicep), and enough strength in my back, shoulders, stomach, and left leg to gain the necessary leverage to make the transfer.

Leverage to a cripple is everything. Leverage takes the place of normal legs, arms, and fingers. Using leverage I was able to wash myself, shave, brush my teeth, comb my hair, and dress myself—just like real people.

Almost from the beginning of my work life at the "Daily News," I began to get severe, migraine-type headaches. They were the kind that make you sick to your stomach, or make your eyes shy from light.

After a few months, Jeannie insisted that I see a doctor. Someone recommended Dr. Mark Frees, an internist in Kettering. He examined me, but strangely did not take my blood pressure.

When I got into the car, I said to Jeannie, "You know, the doctor did not take my blood pressure. Is that some new technique when examining a new patient?" We puzzled over that until the follow-up discussion the next week.

"Mr. Range, your blood work is good and your blood pressure registered an excellent 120 over 70," he said as we sat in his office.

"Excuse me Dr. Frees," I said, "I hate to contradict you, but you never took my blood pressure." He was dumbfounded. "Wait one moment," he said, "I need to speak to one of my nurses." He then went out into the hallway. I could hear a conversation that sounded rather tense, but I could not make out the words.

He came back into the office, and said with obvious embarrassment, "Mr. Range, I was doing two physical examinations that day and we seem to have mixed up some of your results with another man's. Let me take your blood pressure right now."

He did so twice, and looked stunned each time. "Mr. Range," he said, "your blood pressure is 235 over 160—that is more than high enough to cause a stroke. It is absolutely essential that you get this prescription filled and begin taking this medicine immediately."

With that he apologized profusely. The medicine pushed the dangerously high blood pressure readings down to acceptable levels within a few days.

The headaches continued.

Two weeks after I began working at the "Daily News," McLean arrived to take over the copy desk operation. He was a workaholic, an absolute masochist for taking on more responsibility. He often gave me a ride to work in the morning, and always worked Saturday nights, as did I. Later, my early morning driver became Don Timmons, assistant news editor and one of Indiana's finest sons from Logansport, home of the Fighting Berries.

Not only did McLean perform monumental deeds of editing news copy, he did double duty as a firefighter.

Sitting next to me one morning was an anachronism—an aging itinerant copy editor by the name of Jack Ellis. He was tall and pear-shaped, with a large belly stuck on a thin frame. For years, men such as he had traveled from newspaper to newspaper seeking copy-editing work. They rarely stayed long in one place. In some cases, they were trying to stay a step ahead of alimony lawyers. In other cases, alcoholism did them in, or there were darker issues.

In any event, McLean had hired Ellis. He was sitting next to me chain smoking as he edited. Between us was one of those green industrial-strength wastebaskets. Ellis had been throwing lighted cigarette butt after lighted cigarette butt into the wastebasket.

"WHOOSH!"

A giant flame erupted from the wastebasket. Ellis jumped up to escape the huge flame, and in so doing he knocked the basket with its roaring flame against the right arm rest of my wheelchair. I tried to lean away from the ravenous flames that were licking at my arm.

McLean leaped up over his desk and onto mine. He tried to give the basket with its roaring mini-inferno a mighty kick. His kick was slightly off target and his leg went down into the mini-inferno. His momentum knocked the wastebasket backward though, and that got me, and him, out of immediate danger.

A resourceful reporter named Charley Stough, a former Peace Corps volunteer who was unflappable in all manners of human endeavor, rushed up with a fire extinguisher and put out the fire. He also coated my right side with foam, but a damp right side is far preferable to one with third-degree burns. McLean ruined an expensive pair of pants, and lost some hair on his leg, but otherwise he was unscathed physically.

McLean fired the itinerant copy editor not long after the fire incident. Ellis lived in a hotel on the corner near the newspaper building. Jeannie and I kept him supplied with cold cuts, peanut butter, crackers, bread, cookies, and beer for a few weeks. Ellis, who had emphysema, kept talking about needing some money to get to a Veterans Administration hospital near Pittsburgh, where he had some vague kind of relative.

We gave him $600 to get to Pittsburgh. In truth, it was not totally altruistic. He had become a bit of a nuisance. I felt that after dodging one brush with terror in the newsroom, prudence was the better part of valor.

There are two physical dangers that cripples fear above all others: the first is fire, and the second is large dogs.

I do not know if my difficulty in adjusting to the job was the fast pace and heavy work load, the inability to fine-tune my biological clock to a mainly early-day work schedule, a perceived loss of status, or a combination of all those.

While I was pondering those things over a cup of half-finished coffee on one of my off days in early spring 1974, Jeannie said, "We're going to have our third baby in October."

"I know what you're doing, God," I said to myself, "you're punishing me for watching that pornographic movie on the wall of my graduate-student apartment back in 1967."

I felt something had to be done about my work life soon or I would become more and more miserable. In the process I would make life miserable for my sweet wife and our gorgeous children.

I asked for a three-month leave of absence. The company quickly granted it without any questions.

It is easy now to see that I was not using the proper strategies to cope with the increasing pressures. Instead of gearing back and letting life come to me, I was using the old Warm Springs strategy of "Attack, attack, attack."

Maybe my severance from the "Plain Dealer" had so hurt me so badly that I felt that I had to reinvent myself all over again— Jerry Range, Super Gimp.

If I had simply eased off the throttle and not thought that I had to prove that I was a super human masquerading as a cripple, then I might have been in better shape emotionally and mentally.

I could have paced myself—for instance, taking a little bit more time on each piece of news copy and thereby cutting down my work load a bit. Thus I might have saved a significant amount of energy over a week's time. None of my superiors at the "Daily News" ever pressed me to produce at the frenetic pace I thought was necessary.

I now know that the person putting pressure on me was Jerry Range.

I certainly was not a good example of grace under fire. For that, one only needed to look to my young wife who performed incredible feats that went unnoticed and unrewarded. For instance, in the dead of winter with snow on the ground and the temperatures in the teens, she would get up about 4 a.m. in order to get me up at 4:30 a.m.

She would help me get out of bed, set me up to wash and shave in the bathroom while she went about the business of preparing herself to get me to work. When it was time to go, she would go out and start the car in the parking lot about 20 yards from our apartment door. Then she would take me out through the snow, help me get into the car and then fold and stow the wheelchair in the trunk.

She would hurry back into the apartment, bundle up our oldest child, Mickie, then 3, do the same with Jerry Jr., then 1 1/2, and hurry out to the car with both of them.

Then she would drive the nine miles downtown to 45 Ludlow Street, site of the "Daily News" building. She would then get me out of the car and into the wheelchair, and put me inside the lobby.

All this while she was pregnant with Mary Rose. By any definition, that is grace under fire.

I was making family decisions unilaterally. I told Jeannie that we should visit her brother John and his wife Jan in Roswell, Ga., just north of Atlanta. We did that in April 1974, the first month of my leave of absence.

Soon after we got to Roswell, I telephoned the managing editor at the Atlanta "Journal," sister paper to the "Dayton Daily News." Both papers were in the Cox chain, which had been started in Dayton by onetime governor of Ohio, James Cox, who in 1920 was the Democratic presidential nominee. His vice presidential running mate was Franklin D. Roosevelt.

After the death of Cox, company headquarters were moved to Atlanta, where both the morning paper, the "Journal" and the "Constitution" were owned and operated out of the same building. In Dayton, the "Daily News" and our "sister" morning paper the "Journal-Herald" likewise operated out of the same building.

The managing editor at the Atlanta "Journal" granted me a short interview. I never heard from him again. I turned my attention to the daily newspaper published in Marietta, Ga., about 15 miles northwest of Atlanta. Again, the editor there said I could come in for an interview.

Jeannie and I went right through the middle of their small newsroom to the stupefied stares of their news staff. A woman who identified herself as the editor's personal secretary showed us into an empty room with a bare table and chairs. She excused herself, and came back in about two or three minutes holding the resume I had sent.

"Y'all don't want to work here," she said. "They are incredibly cheap here, and believe me when I say that y'all won't be happy here. In fact, I just got a new job and can't wait to get out of here."

"Do you still want to talk to the editor?" she asked.

"With that ringing endorsement, I guess not," I said. "But what about the ring of suburban dailies that this place owns?" I asked.

"Even cheaper," she said, "much cheaper." With that, we took our leave. My final shot in Georgia was at the Columbus paper. Columbus is on Georgia's western border with Alabama. I had sent a resume there also. When I called, the managing editor said, "I see what y'all are makin' in Dayton, and we can't come anywhere near that; not even close."

"So do you want me to come down for an interview?" I said. "Y'all are welcome to come down, but ah think it would be a waste of time." That was that.

I did not want the Georgia experience to be a total failure, so we drove down to Warm Springs, 85 miles southwest of Atlanta. I showed Jeannie the beautiful campus-like grounds of the Foundation, and we even slipped into the area where I had stayed as a patient.

We ate in the dining hall at Georgia Hall, which was still governed by the same immaculately dressed black maitre d'. He still ruled entry by the same rigid system: patients first, staff second, relatives and other visitors third.

I had hoped to introduce Jeannie to Grace Marie Freyman, the woman who had been so influential in seeing that I got a first-class college education. She had convinced me that I could succeed in life despite living in a wheelchair and having only "half" of an arm to survive on.

An old friend on the administrative staff told me that Miss Freyman had returned to her native Iowa to attend to her ailing sister after nearly three decades at Warm Springs. She never returned to Warm Springs.

By now we had spent nearly a month in Georgia, mostly sponging off my in-laws. I had rolled the dice in Georgia, and had lost.

We went down to Jacksonville, Fla., where I interviewed at the morning newspaper. There were no job openings, but I left my resume with the managing editor. After another six or seven weeks, I went back to work on the copy desk in Dayton.

I became moodier at home, and demanded perfection from Jeannie.

At work, I kept up a facade of cheerfulness. My wife and children were beginning to pay the price of my unhappiness.

The job at the "Daily News" presented me with an unusual challenge. Prior to Dayton, I would simply set my sights on a goal and then charge ahead like a tank until I had crushed all obstacles and had attained that goal. At the "Daily News" all I could see was an unending series of frenzied days stretching beyond the horizon.

One Saturday afternoon when I came in, McLean was standing over to the left of the multi-metal-desk "copy desk."

On the floor nearby was a taped diagram of the new copy desk, with designated squares for the new VDTs (video display terminals). McLean said, "Jerry, here's your new home." He pushed me over to the front left portion of the oblong-shaped diagram.

Soon we were doing all of our editing on the VDTs. On the one hand, the new technology freed me from the drudgery of the lead-bar system of cut and paste. On the other hand, the VDTs did exactly what their designers had told the company they would.

It is easy to imagine what the first meeting with the representatives of the Hendrix Co., maker of the computers, and executives from Dayton Newspapers Inc. was like.

"Are you trying to tell us that by buying 100 VDTs at a cost of $600,000 we are actually going to save money?" our bosses asked.

"Absolutely," the Hendrix representatives said. "Over time, you will see that your individual editors will be handling at least 20 percent more news copy per editor than in the past. You will be able to slow down hiring by not replacing full-time people who leave. We estimate that you'll recover the entire cost of the system well before the five-year life span of the machines is up."

The technocrats were right on the money.

For instance, there were many Saturday nights when McLean and I were the editing staff. God Himself only knows how many stories I edited on those nights. On one night when I kept a log, I reached the mid-'30s. After that, I stopped counting. That is an incredible amount of news copy handled by one person in less than eight hours.

So the new VDTs—the wonder machines of the New Age in newspapering—liberated me physically, while locking me and thousands of others into higher levels of production.

A year after the computers came, there was a new "hire" on the desk, a young woman named Ann Berry. I was the prototypical male chauvinist pig. She was a Cincinnati native, a graduate of an all-girls' Catholic high school in Cincinnati, and was an alumnus of Marshall University in Huntington, W.Va.

She had worked in Las Cruces, NM, and in Morristown, Tenn.

"Why would they hire such an obviously ill-prepared young woman?" I asked myself. My problem was that I had started at the top in Ohio newspapering—the "Plain Dealer." I did not realize that simply being on the staff and collecting a paycheck at such a place meant that I was a major-league copy editor.

Berry, on the other hand, had more than paid her dues. She was enormously efficient, well-organized at everything she undertook, and incredibly good at editing news copy. She soon became assistant copy desk chief. She became copy desk chief when McLean was promoted to metropolitan editor. It did not take me long to recognize that she was a damn fine copy editor.

Jeannie and I soon began taking her home to her rented house in East Dayton after the Saturday night shift. And I began regarding her as the younger sister I had always wanted and had never had.

Down through the next 15 years, we worked closely together and I believe a genuine affection grew between us. I still value that.

While McLean and Berry were working in tandem as copy desk chief and assistant copy desk chief respectively, I decided to learn only enough to be able to edit efficiently. Berry on the other hand poured herself into learning all there was to know about computers in the newspaper business.

Production at my home was on schedule also. Mary Rose was born on Oct. 10, 1974. I was beginning to look upon the children and their demands on me when I was home as a burden instead of an escape from the pressure of work.

I was far too heavy on the discipline and far too light on the joy and laughter. Worst of all, I was placing the blame for the continuing deluge of children on Jeannie—as if I had nothing to do with it.

From me, Jeannie needed adult conversation and participation in adult activities, even if vicariously in my work life. I did not give enough of that part of my life to her. Also, she needed me to be more of a presence in my children's lives. Instead, I demanded that she make the household run perfectly as we produced more children.

I was not a good father, or a helpful husband. Nevertheless, my children gave me unconditional love.

To reach for things, I had developed a simple technique of holding the cuff of my right sleeve in my teeth and extending my right arm. I did it in the newsroom, and after the initial shock wore off, the staff ignored it.

When each one of my children was about two or three years of age, he or she would lift their right arm by holding their sleeves in their teeth. Imitation is the greatest form of flattery. It also is a great expression of love.

After the third child was born, my father said, "Jer, you'd better do something about getting yourself 'fixed'. You guys simply have too many children."

"Sure, Dad, you're right about that."

Then when Christopher was in incubation inside Jeannie in 1976, my parents apparently decided that I had become the village idiot, and they said no more about it. However, I told Jeannie, "We really have to do something about more children. I'm going to make an appointment with a urologist to have a vasectomy done."

My ideology had been evolving right-ward since the Roe v. Wade decision legalized abortion in 1973. When I went for my interview with the urologist, I was totally split in my own mind. I was a Catholic who respected the church's position on things like sterilization. On the other hand, I felt enormous pressure because of our growing family. The prospects of even more than four were more than realistic.

In the discussion with the urologist, I somehow worked into the dialogue—and I have no idea how this happened—the fact that Hitler had forced people to be sterilized.

"I'm no Nazi!" the startled doctor shouted. Somehow we got through the interview, and set a date and time for the vasectomy. He probably thought I needed a frontal lobotomy.

On the day before the procedure, Jeannie said, "Jerry, you've gone through so much. I don't want to see you have more pain. Please don't do it."

"Honey, if that is what you really want, then that is what I will do. I still think that I should do it, but I respect your wishes."

I did not have the vasectomy.

In 1975, I took my best shot at finding a teaching job. I was a subscriber to the magazine "Editor & Publisher," the so-called "Bible" of the newspaper industry. Every week in "E&P" there were ads for newspaper job openings and also ads for journalism teachers.

I interviewed for a job at Indiana State University in Terre Haute, Ind. I came in second. The man who interviewed me recommended me for a job at a small girl's college just north of Terre Haute called St. Mary's of the Woods. The nun who was the president of the school of about 900 young women needed someone to teach a seminar-type class in journalism writing, and to edit the school's literary quarterly.

It seemed like manna from heaven until I heard the salary offer. She offered $10,000 a year. At that time I was making a little bit more than $17,000 a year at the "Daily News."

Over the phone, I told her, "Sister, if you can make it $12,000, I will take it."

"Give me a day and I will get back to you."

She could offer no more money. I had a wife and three children. I would be cutting my income by nearly 40 percent. It simply could not be done.

I was not then a militant cripple, nor am I one now. However, a letter I got from the head of the search committee at Western Kentucky State University made me boil over. In all my letters, I felt I was ethically bound to say upfront that I was in a wheelchair.

He wrote back saying in part, "Our campus is very hilly, and we hold most of our journalism staff meetings in a building on top of a hill. You would find it difficult navigating our campus."

I immediately shot a letter back to him saying, "If you want to hire a cross-country runner to teach journalism to your students, then hire such an athlete. On the other hand, if you want to hire someone qualified both academically and in terms of experience, I am your man. I don't give a damn about your hill. I can do the job."

He must have feared a lawsuit, because on a Sunday about 8 p.m. he called me and profusely apologized. My anger was assuaged, but I did not get the job. The Americans with Disabilities Act came about 20 years too late.

The managing editor of the morning newspaper in Jacksonville, the "Florida Times-Union," called and offered me an interview. On the coldest day in the history of Dayton, Ohio, with the mercury at—25 Fahrenheit, my dad and I flew out of Dayton to Jacksonville.

The next day in Jacksonville it warmed up in the afternoon to 57 degrees Fahrenheit. Back in Dayton, it was still far below zero. The managing editor offered me a job at $12,000. They would not pay for my move.

"Give me a few days to think about it, would you please?" I asked him.

"Take all the time y'all want," he said.

Back home in the apartment, I talked it over with Jeannie. Once again, I turned down Jacksonville's sunshine for Ohio's cold dollars.

I resigned myself to the fact that we were going to be in Dayton for the rest of our lives.

A few months later in the spring of 1976, Jeannie said with hesitation and fear in her voice, "Jerry, we're going to have another baby." I should have been overjoyed. The news depressed me greatly.

She was creating miracles, and I was figuratively crying like the little miracles she produced, with some small help from me, of course.

I still had some of my wits about me, and so we began to look for a house to buy. We found a three-bedroom ranch with a large patio, and a secluded backyard on the east side of Kettering. The price in the fall of 1977 was $44,500. It had a two-car attached garage, and a working fireplace.

About this time I got help from news editor Beyer. When I told him of my difficulty in getting up early, he said, "Well, let's do something about that. Instead of coming in at 6 a.m., why not come in at 8:30?"

In addition, the copy desk was reorganized and I became the designated copy editor on the "God squad." That was our term for the makeup person and the copy editor who on Fridays prepared in advance Sunday's business section, and filled some other back pages in the Sunday paper. Chuck Pettee, Ann Berry's future husband, was my boss on that shift.

For that shift on Fridays, I came in at 10 a.m., and worked until 6 p.m. In addition, I became the designated copy editor for special projects.

Three come to mind:

In 1975, a federal judge ordered the Dayton city schools to desegregate all schools under a court-ordered busing plan. The plan affected about 31,000 students.

Copy editor Dennis Polite and I were named the designated copy editors on the "deseg" edition. Polite was incredibly well-informed, and incredibly black. I was not so well-informed and incredibly Caucasian. We had two things in common: we were both copy editors, and we were both Catholic.

Otherwise, we had little in common except mutual respect.

In the late 1970s, one of the many bosses had a brainstorm called "Facing the' 80's." It involved enormously long stories—about as exciting as reading the dictionary—and pictures predicting what would happen in the Dayton area in the coming decade.

Another special project that I worked on was the commemorative edition of the great 1913 flood in Dayton. The entire downtown had been covered by water. Legendary Daytonian John H. Patterson, owner and operator of National Cash Register Co. (now NCR Corp.), "saved" the city by converting his huge factory to the production of flat-bottomed boats which were maneuvered around to rescue people from the second stories of their homes, and to bring others food and fresh water.

Another "cripple," Dean Lyndoerfer, laid out the pages. I did the copy editing. Lyndoerfer nearly was a pseudo-cripple. He used a short leg brace as a result of polio. People in the newsroom ridiculed him behind his back for what was perceived as his bootlicking manner. I had no problem with him, except when he tried to write cutlines (picture captions). He was terrible at it. He was good at designing pages, but his flair did not extend to writing.

All the external pieces seemed to be falling into place for me to have a happy life in Dayton, Ohio, by the end of 1977. However, slowly and steadily, I was deteriorating inside. I could not communicate that deterioration to anyone, not even to Jeannie.

End of Chapter 9

CHAPTER 10

"Lewd Dances, Big 'Sis' Clara, No Miracles"

By the late '70s my schedule had been modified to the point where I was working about 32 hours a week as a copy editor. But even after nearly seven years there, I still felt the necessity to prove myself.

I wanted to write, and the main opportunity open to me was doing book reviews. On occasion, I would offer "op-ed" pieces trying to refute what our liberal local columnists had written.

The opportunity to write such pieces was infrequent. More and more my need to be creative found its only outlet in what were called "lines for wild art." Typically, a photographer would be instructed to go out and shoot a picture of, for instance, the first snowfall of the season. The picture would be sized and placed in the page design by someone on the news desk. Then it was up to a copy editor to look at the generic piece of art and write a caption for it.

With more and more frequency, Ann (by now it was Ann Pettee) would give those little jobs to me. It was a challenge to look at a picture and give the reader something he could not see in the picture, something that I hoped would be almost poetic.

I felt that I needed much more than those kinds of challenges.

I had known internal turmoil since my body stopped to function properly at age 11. That inner turmoil never stopped. Few people other than my wife Jeannie knew that. Over the years, she grew closer and closer to God. Meanwhile, I was fighting a closer relationship with God every step of the way.

Other people seem to glide through life effortlessly while everything I achieved had come through huge expenditures of effort and energy.

How have I reconciled my severe crippling with a loving God? I haven't. In fact, Jeannie has said to me, "When you see God in heaven, will you ask for an explanation?"

"I don't think anyone will be bold enough to stand in front of God and say, 'Why?'" I replied.

Why did that loving God do this to me? He did, or maybe he did not. There is the ticklish problem of free will. If my parents had not decided to take a week's vacation at the little lake in Pennsylvania where we had gone for many years, would I have gotten poliomyelitis? I don't know.

Why did none of the other five or six children in the two families who shared one large cottage get the disease? I don't know.

Did God take a hand in these things? I do not know. Chance, circumstance, randomness, or some inexplicable Grand Design? I DO NOT KNOW.

So it comes full circle: you deal with the cards that you are dealt, and I do that. But that does not mean I like the hand that I have.

My son Peter and my son-in-law Mike went with me to an Indians ballgame in Cleveland. Other than the fact that the Indians lost, with 41,000 in the stands it was a great spectacle, but I had difficulty enjoying the spectacle.

My body hurt like hell. Besides the usual pains from my crooked back, my right hip, which for 32 years has had that steel rod in it after the automobile accident, ached like an abscessed tooth when ice cold water pours over it.

It does that often at inopportune times. I could not relax, and I could not communicate that inability to relax to anyone else, because there was nothing anyone could do about it. It certainly did not qualify as suffering; that word is meant for truly gruesome things. I call it "extreme discomfort."

I rather doubt that God planned for me to be extremely uncomfortable. But it happens almost on a daily basis, and after 46 years as a cripple such things still can make me angry.

After the game, we were heading to our parking lot. A down-and-out black man called out for some money.

Peter said, "I'm sorry, I'm all-out."

The man then saw me in the wheelchair that Peter was pushing, and said, "Don't worry about it, buddy, you guys have a good night."

He was feeling momentarily sorry for me. Undoubtedly, his life story was one of true suffering—the pain of which was probably dulled when he could buy booze.

Paradox is built into life. God loves me, but he allows pain and me to be intimate. When I reached my 40s, all the struggling, all the mountains climbed, and all the pain I had endured were all proving to be too much.

Such things get internalized. Any doctor worth his diploma will say that internal stress and strain eventually leads to symptoms like migraine headaches, upset stomachs, acid reflux, ulcers, or maybe diarrhea. "One way or other," Dr. Frees once told me, "severe stress will show itself in physical symptoms." I had them all.

I dutifully saw that my children saw their father going to church. But for many years in the late '70s and early '80s, that was probably the only reason I went to mass.

My love/hate relationship with God was frightening to Jeannie. So it was a great blessing when an angel in human form stepped into our lives just after we got the house in late 1977. The angel's name was Clara Muzechuk.

About the time that we bought the house, the nearest Catholic church, St. Charles, installed a ramp in the front of the church. After a mass in the late fall of '77, Jeannie was trying to get all the kids into their coats, hats, and gloves. A slim woman came up to us. She had close-cropped black hair just starting to gray at the edges framing large brown glasses that magnified her soft welcoming eyes. She had a small nose, and a wide mouth with soft sensuous lips that broke easily into a smile.

"You seem to need a little bit of help with these little guys," she said to Jeannie. She helped Jeannie get the four kids ready for the out of doors. The next thing we knew she had become a vital part of our lives and the lives of our children in Kettering.

She became a second mother to our children. The ones that were in school went to her house after the school day was over, because her own six-child family lived near the church and school. It was the kind of house where everyone was welcomed, especially children.

She came along at a time when Jeannie was in great need of a female friend. I was becoming more and more withdrawn at home. Clara's late husband Dick, who held a number of engineering patents for the Inland Division of General Motors, was used to his attractive wife bringing home people who needed help.

Later on, Dick and I would team together in a fantasy baseball league directed by "Daily News" sportswriter Gary Nuhn. Dick was a stickler for details, and read the "Sporting News" religiously. In the first year of the fantasy league the team of RangeMuze cleaned the clocks of many of Dayton's sports elite. We split a pot worth $600.

Many of our kids were in the same grades at St. Charles School, and later at Archbishop Alter High School. Our kids probably ate more of Clara's food then they did of ours. She was always smiling, and she was always hugging. Jeannie and the kids loved her, and still do. After I had known her half a dozen years, I said, "Clara, would you be my older sister? I always needed and wanted an older sister."

"Sure I would, Handsome!" she said with that wonderfully shining smile and a warm kiss on the cheek.

So I gained an older sister.

I was always setting myself up for a fall. Soon after we moved into the house, I wrote to the managing editor of the Cincinnati "Enquirer." He set up a time for an interview, and Jeannie and I went down to Cincinnati. The "Enquirer" was a morning paper. That meant that I would be working from late afternoon to around midnight. I figured that it would at least give me the chance to get the sleep I needed. It was becoming harder for me to get to sleep. Often I was going on three or four hours of sleep at night.

The managing editor, Jim Shuttlekotte, was the brother of locally famed Cincinnati news telecaster Al Shuttlekotte. The managing editor indicated that I was hired by suggesting that I look in northern Kentucky for a place to live just across the Ohio River from downtown Cincinnati. He said that there was a pro forma physical exam done at a clinic in downtown Cincinnati. We went there, and I had a cursory exam. Three weeks went by without my hearing from Shuttlekotte.

Finally I called him, and asked, "Why haven't you called me with a time to start to work?"

"Hasn't the personnel director called you?" he said.

"No," I said in a puzzled voice.

"Well, she will be calling you," he said.

She did that afternoon, and said that the urine test had revealed a trace of diabetes. I immediately went to Dr. Frees, who was an internist skilled in the diagnosis and treatment of diabetes. Dr. Frees ran a series of tests on me and said that there was no trace of diabetes. "However," he said, "this drug you've been taking for hypertension can give a false-positive reading for diabetes."

I called Shuttlekotte in Cincinnati, and told him what my doctor had said.

"I am sorry, but the position has been filled," he said.

"You bastard!" I said. "This is a really shabby way to treat people." I slammed down the phone.

If anything, I grew more intense at work, and harder to get along with at home. To make matters worse, an old scab deep down in some long forgotten recess of my heart ripped open and out came the pain left by the memory of my high school girlfriend, Jacque.

I was ashamed of myself and disgusted that she was back in my thoughts; back like a wound long forgotten that suddenly and inexplicably begins to hurt again.

Here I was—a man with a lovely wife, four loving children, and I could not eliminate from my memory inconsequential things about a woman that I could no longer picture in my mind. It was maddening. The frustration ate away at me like dripping acid. It would be almost 14 years before someone could put that memory in perspective and end the frustration.

One of the things I was never able to accomplish was to form a lasting, close friendship with another man. I was on a friendly basis with dozens of men, but there was no one who understood me. Most of the guys at work had friends with whom they played golf 10 months of the year, or tennis in the warmer months. I would listen to them scheduling their golf games, or their tennis matches, and I would say to myself, "God, I would give a year of my life to be able to play 18 holes of golf with any of these guys."

I would daydream at work of how it might have been shooting hoops with my kids, playing football with Jerry Jr. and Christopher in the backyard, or playing catch with Peter, who wanted to be a good baseball player.

All I could do was offer advice, and I later found that to be worth only the air on which the words are said. After one of Peter's Little League games, I began my usual post-game critique.

"Dad," Peter said, "why do you always have to be criticizing the things I did in the game? Why can't you just let me play it?"

That took guts, because all my kids knew that I had a hair-trigger temper and while I posed no physical danger to them, my words could cut like razor blades.

I was becoming more and more morose. I wanted to do something significant. I wanted to prove to people in my world—to my former bosses in Cleveland and to my new bosses in Dayton, to my parents, to my co-workers in Dayton, and to my wife that what I was doing had meaning and significance.

All my wife wanted was a husband who could give her support and comfort; who could help her with the kids; who could share her deepening faith in God. I wanted to be a star. In her eyes, I already was one.

By the early '80s, I had lost some functioning ability, particularly the ability to get in and to get out of bed or on and off the toilet without help. That was born of necessity—to have enough time to get ready in the morning for work, I could not spend 20 minutes getting out of bed by myself.

So on a typical workday, Jeannie would help me get out of bed and push me out to the kitchen for a quick breakfast. Then she would take me to the back bathroom, where I would wash myself, shave, and brush my teeth. Meanwhile, she would be getting the school-age children ready for the bus. She would take time out to help me get onto the raised seat that I used over the commode.

Soon the kids would be off to school, and she would get me off the commode. Then she would help me get dressed. I could still lift my rump off the seat of the wheelchair by hooking my shoulder blades over the back panel and lifting up my hips. She then could slide the pants up over my hips and gut.

Then Jeannie would drive me to downtown Dayton. Until 1981, she still had Christopher at home, and like any small child, he required attention. She would drive down at 3 p.m., pick me up and take me back home. All this might have come after a night when I had demanded lovemaking. When I got home, often the dishes were not washed, or the table was not cleaned off.

"Why do you let these chores pile up?" I would say sharply. She held her tongue and did not tell me how tired she was. In the late afternoon, she would drive over to Clara's house and pick up the older children. Then she would make dinner, wash the kids' school clothing, and help them if they had special projects and needed something for school from the store, or if they simply needed help with their homework. I did help some with the kids' homework, and I did read to them when they were small.

By 8 p.m., she would often fall asleep in a living room chair. My reaction was, "If she only were more organized, she wouldn't get so tired." I was selfish. I lacked compassion.

Not only did I not help, I was part of the problem.

I was concentrating on externals. I thought that by having an electric wheelchair at work, I would be able to get away from the desk to give myself mental health breaks. At first, we thought that we would leave the chair at work parked in the photo studio. However, we worried that someone might find the temptation to fiddle with the chair too tempting, so we had to come up with a means of transporting it.

We went to Roger Flint, who was in a wheelchair himself from a neuro-muscular disease. He ran a van conversion shop. We did not have enough money to buy a new van, so we bought a 6-year-old Plymouth van equipped with a wheelchair lift from Flint, who said it was a great buy. Immediately after we took possession, the brakes went out. Only by the grace of God and the fact that we were on Clara's prayer list did Jeannie and the kids escape serious injury.

We had another close call with the used van. On a chilly autumn day Jeannie, who was then five months pregnant in 1981, was taking me to work with all four of the other children in the van. We were going up Woodman Drive, a four-lane north-south artery that led to U.S. 35, the freeway that cut through East Dayton into downtown.

Just before reaching the freeway, we heard "Pop, Pop, Pop" coming from under the van.

"Turn left into that residential area," I told Jeannie. As we did, the popping noise intensified and then suddenly as we rolled down the residential street, there was an explosion from under the hood, and the van began filling with smoke. Jeannie stopped in front of a house.

I yelled: "You big kids, grab the little ones and get out, NOW!" They all got out quickly.

Jeannie quickly undid my "lockdowns," the devices that kept the wheelchair from moving about in the van. I moved between the front seats. Jeannie pulled me onto the right front seat. A woman who had been watching came running with a lawn chair. Pregnant Jeannie dragged me down out of the van and onto the lawn chair. Another woman came running with some sand and opened up the van's hood and threw it on to the battery, which was on fire. That stopped the fire.

It was just another example, a powerful one, of Jeannie's grace under fire—literally.

For the seven years that we had the van, it must have been in and out of the repair shop a dozen times for major repairs costing enormous sums. That van had a great deal to do with our ever-increasing financial problems.

The Regional Transit Authority introduced a door-to-door service for severely handicapped people. I qualified. The bus would stop right at the bottom of our driveway, and take me to the "Daily News" building.

For two years, the RTA's "targeted" system gave Jeannie some relief from a difficult chore. Unfortunately, militant cripples in Dayton demanded complete access to the bus system instead of a targeted system. They said a targeted system stereotyped them. They proved that being crippled does not make one smart.

The RTA said it was either a targeted system or a massive integration of the entire bus fleet. The militants won. The serious cripples like myself who needed a targeted system were turned over to a taxi company that leased with RTA funds an aging fleet of mini-buses from a company in Columbus. Also, RTA pulled out of the service drivers who had been trained in handling severely crippled people. We were left with totally untrained people making minimum wage.

One night after work one of the mini-buses stopped in front of the "Daily News" building. Out jumped one of the Hatfields or maybe it was one of the McCoys. He said, "Ah kinda don't know ma way 'round Dayton. Kin y'all tell me how to get to Smithville Road?"

"Sure," I said, as I showed him how to load me on the rickety old mini-bus. When I got on, there was a young lady in a wheelchair on the vehicle. She worked at the Dayton Power & Light Co. building a few blocks from the newspaper building.

She looked frightened enough to cry. I used some light-hearted conversation to try to ease her fear. The driver got on and said, "Would you mind if I stopped at my grandmother's house? She has some food for me."

What choice did we have? We stopped outside of a house in East Dayton. When the "driver" returned, the smell of alcohol was unmistakable. I directed him to the young woman's apartment building, and then directed him to my house in Kettering.

After getting off and entering the house, I said to Jeannie, "I am sorry, but that is the last time I will ride RTA's so-called service."

In 1982, I had a horrendous medical experience that only added to my already-plunging spirits. For about 10 days, I had a throat infection. The antibiotics prescribed by the doctor seemed to have no effect. I woke up one morning and felt something "furry" on the roof of my mouth. I asked Jeannie to look at it.

"I don't know what it is, but it doesn't look good. We better get you to the doctor." I was in one of his examining rooms about 3:30 in the afternoon. As soon as Dr. Frees saw the "furry" spot, he said, "My God, I haven't seen something like this in 25 years!" He stepped out into the hallway, and shouted to his nurse, "Come look at this!"

He said, "This is an abscess and it could go to your brain. You must have it drained right away." He called an ear/nose/throat specialist in downtown Dayton, a Dr. Bickmore.

He came back into the examining room and said, "Dr. Bickmore has cleared his schedule and will see you immediately." So we drove through a thunderstorm to a medical office building downtown. We went into a huge waiting room filled with patients.

When we introduced ourselves to the receptionist, she said, "Dr. Bickmore will see you immediately." She led us back through an area where there were about 10 examining rooms all filled with ear/nose/throat specialists.

When Dr. Bickmore came in, he immediately examined my mouth. He said, "That abscess must be drained immediately. Unfortunately, it is in a place where I cannot give you an anesthetic."

He went to a drawer and withdrew a silver instrument that had a hideous-looking sharp pick on the end. He said, "I'm not going to kid you. This is going to hurt."

He was right on the money.

He had me tilt my head back. He began to dig into the roof of my mouth. Never had I known such pain. Not from anything that polio had done to me, nor from any pain from the accident in Cleveland when I fractured so many bones. He dug around, and foul-looking brown liquid gushed out. I expelled it into a plastic receptacle. Tears were streaming down my face. Jeannie later told me that I had turned ashen white.

He said, "I am sorry, but we have to go in one more time." Again, pain the likes of which I never knew existed exploded in my mouth. Then it was over.

"You must get your tonsils out, or the same kind of abscess could reappear," he said.

For three weeks after the surgery, I could swallow nothing but bits of Popsicles. When we saw Dr. Bickmore for the postoperative session, he said that because of my incredibly stiff neck he was only able to get one tonsil out. He said, "But I had the temerity to continue and I got the second one out also." I had never heard anyone use the word "temerity" in conversation until then.

Not long after I got back to work, I used a bit of temerity myself, or more accurately, a little bit of fast thinking. One morning when I was fiercely working on the first edition, I became aware of someone at my left elbow. I continued another minute or two to bang away on the VDT keyboard.

Finally, the person next to me began to mumble. I stopped editing and turned toward him. It was a thin young man who was shabbily dressed. He needed a shave and obviously a shower. His old sport coat was threadbare and stained. He had opened a briefcase that had obviously been filled in purposeful order with leaflets and notepads with handwritten notes on them.

He said in a monotone, "They have planted a radio receiver in my brain, and they are making me do lewd dances."

"Excuse me, sir," I said, "what did you say?"

He repeated in that monotone: "They have planted a radio receiver in my brain, and they are making me do lewd dances."

"Oh, my God, have I got a live one here," I said to myself.

I told him, "Sir, I do not make policy decisions. I am just an ordinary worker. The man who will be able to help solve your problem is right over there wearing the white shirt with the blue and gray tie." (I pointed to Steve Sidlo, the city editor).

The young man carefully folded all of his material and just as carefully put it back in the "proper" places in the worn-out briefcase. He then shut the briefcase, thanked me, and went over to the city editor. He sat down, opened his briefcase, and began to speak.

Sidlo looked at him, and then looked at me. Sidlo mouthed the words across the noisy newsroom, "You son of a bitch!"

"Security" at that time at the "Daily News" consisted of calling Harvey Knuckles, a short burly member of the maintenance crew. Sidlo had carefully picked up the phone with his right hand after listening to the young man seated to his left. Knuckles arrived carrying a sledgehammer. He escorted the young man out of the building.

Soon after that, the "Daily News" hired a security firm to screen people who entered the lobbies.

Soon after that episode, I was waiting for Jeannie outside the building on the corner. A nondescript man in late middle age, and shabbily dressed, was mumbling incoherently to himself as he walked by me. He stopped, turned toward me and grabbed my "good" right thumb and began to try to break it by forcing it backwards.

I managed to hit the control stick on the wheelchair with my forearm, thus forcing the wheelchair to plow forward into him. That caused him to release my thumb.

He said, "Hey, buddy, you got 50 cents?"

He then turned and crossed the street against the light.

That incident was symbolic of my state of mind and heart. Life seemed ever more chaotic and useless. It is difficult to explain why despite all the human warmth around me, life was losing any sense of purpose. I was hurting my wife and children. Our fifth child, Peter, had arrived on Dec. 22, 1981. Patrick followed on Nov. 15, 1983.

Just before Patrick's birth, Jeannie talked to a good friend who was a priest in the Cleveland Diocese. He told her, "If you want to have a husband to help you raise the six children you now have, sterilization is your only choice." About a half-hour after Patrick was born, we both signed the consent form for Jeannie's sterilization. Only her signature was necessary, but I told her, "We were one when the children were created; we should be one now."

Both of us have long since received absolution in the Sacrament of Reconciliation (Confession), but I still believe that the lion's share of the guilt lies with me. My loving wife Jeannie did it for me, because she feared I could not handle having any more children.

By now I had refinanced the house four times. I seemed to be sinking deeper and deeper into a hole of no escape.

There was no sunshine in my life. Life was like chewing metal. I began to think of suicide.

Jeannie told Clara about my problems.

There was a charismatic Catholic priest from Massachusetts who had achieved a reputation as a faith healer. He was to appear at Precious Blood Church on Dayton's northwest side. With the purest of intentions, Clara got Jeannie to agree to take me to the service.

When Jeannie brought the subject up, I was angry, but I held Clara in such high regard that I agreed to go. When we got to the church, the parking lot was overflowing and people attending the service parked in the parking lot of the Salem Mall across the street.

There was a crowd of people blocking the front doorway to the church. "Good," I said to myself, "I will not have to go in." But when the people who were standing in the doorway saw me, the crowd parted like the Red Sea had for Moses.

I was hauled up the steps and led through the jam-packed church to the front where there were 30 or so people in wheelchairs, on stretchers, and standing on braces and crutches. I was in the second row of cripples with Jeannie immediately behind my wheelchair.

The faith-healing priest from Massachusetts came out, led the congregation in prayers and in hymn singing. Then he gave a short talk about God's power to heal.

Then he went to the first line of cripples and people began falling over backwards like trees under attack by a crew of loggers.

"Get me out of here!" I said. "There's no way we can get back through the crowd," Jeannie said.

"I don't care if you have to knock down old ladies!" I said in a panic over my shoulder to her. Somehow, we worked our way back through the crowd. Again the crowd at the doorway parted. Several men took me down the steps.

"Please," I said to Jeannie, "don't ever do that to me again. Tell Clara that I get panicky in crowds, or I can't bear the heat or . . . anything . . ."

I believe in miracles, but I do not believe the miracle of a restored body will happen to me. Put another way, I believe in God, but I just do not know His depth of interest in me.

One afternoon on a very warm day in the summer of 1984 as Jeannie drove me home from work, I told her to go through a drive-through where I bought a six-pack of beer. When we got home, I tossed down a double shot of vodka. I took the six-pack and went out in my electric wheelchair to sit in the shadow of the high bushes at the back of our property. I drank four beers in quick succession.

Then I urinated in my pants.

Later that night, after she had cleaned me up and after I had sobered up, Jeannie said to me, "Jerry, please, you must get help. I can't give you the help you need. And we can't go on like this. I love you, but you're plunging a knife into my heart. And I just can't shield the kids much longer from the same kind of pain. Please go to the County clinic tomorrow."

I agreed to go.

Even I could see that the alternative to getting professional help was a continuing downward spiral—a nosedive that could drag Jeannie and the six kids with me into the hell I was creating.

End of Chapter 10

CHAPTER 11

"Sisyphus, and the Black Beast of Depression"

It felt good to cry again. I had not been able to cry for 20 years. The psychologist started the first session by saying, "What is your problem, and how can I help you?" I had been in his office no more than five minutes when the dam broke, and I sobbed uncontrollably for several minutes.

I had begun by reciting a carefully prepared litany of my troubles. I lost it in a deluge of warm, cleansing tears. I had forgotten just how useful tears could be.

As I sobbed, I tried to apologize to the psychologist. He was leaning back in his chair holding the stem of an unlit pipe in his mouth. Occasionally, he would look at it in a disinterested manner, and return it to his mouth.

This kind of gushing forth was undoubtedly commonplace to him. He probably saw this kind of waterworks several times a week.

Eventually, the tears ended, and the talking began. I told him in abbreviated fashion of my happy childhood, of polio at age 11, and of knowing sleeplessness for the first time in my life. I also told him of the initial onset of paralysis, of how my left arm began to get "heavy" as I sat in a bed in a hospital for patients with contagious diseases.

I told him of being "broiled" on a rubber sheet covered with a cotton sheet upon which were piled steaming "hot packs." I told him that the torture would continue for about 30 minutes as I sweated under the steaming load. Then there would be another 30 minutes after the attendants flipped me over.

"All this was taking place," I told him, "when I still had a temperature of 104+ Fahrenheit." I told him of Zem Zem Hospital, of Warm Springs, and of the 19-month separation from my family.

I laid out for him all the work and all the struggle at the University of Illinois, and at the "Plain Dealer." I told him of all the lonely nights high above the earth, and how I had despaired of finding someone who would love me despite my being crippled.

Then I told him of how my life turned on a dime when a police officer said, "Oh, let's take him to St. John's." I told him of meeting the most beautiful girl with the finest figure, and the brightest smile I had ever seen. I told him that on the very first day that we began to talk to one another, I decided that this was the girl I was going to marry.

For nearly a year I had barely spoken with my wife. I had found that not talking to someone who loves you, not speaking of ordinary things in everyday life, of simply strangling communication, was the worst possible dagger one could plunge into the heart of another. But it was a two-edged dagger—while I was hurting Jeannie, I was also wounding myself.

Now, after the wonderful release of tears, there was another wonderful feeling of release of the words—words disjointed in chronology, all wanting to charge out of my mouth like hyped-up football players after a pep talk in the locker room, ready to break down the door to get out onto the field and get after the opponent.

He stopped me and said, "The hour is up. When can you meet with me again next week?"

I wanted to go on and on, but I had to obey the schedule. So I scheduled an appointment for a week later.

When I got out to the lobby, Jeannie stood up, put down a magazine and said, "How did it go?"

"Honey," I said, "you got me to do the right thing. I feel better already." For the first time in a long time, a sigh of deep relief came past her tender lips. On the way home, I could not stop talking to her about my favorable impressions of the psychoanalyst, my refreshing flood of tears, and my delight in finding someone to whom I could open my heart like street workers open a valve on a fire hydrant to flush out dirt and grime.

I felt as if I were flushing out the dirt, the grime, and the darkness that had crusted over layer after layer, year after year inside of me.

"But I can see that there is a long, long way to go," I said to Jeannie.

"Thank God you at least know there is help available," she said. She turned into a parking lot.

"Why are you stopping here?" I asked.

"Because I am so happy," she said as she laid her head on her hands that were side-by-side on the steering wheel and cried quietly.

All that could be heard inside that cavernous green van was the soft sound of her gentle weeping, and the sound of two hearts once again beating in unison.

I had told the therapist that the main thing that I did to hurt my wife was simply not to speak except in brief, sharp sentences. That had gone on for nearly a year. But there was more. I had done stupid things to both my wife, my children, and even some of their pets. The stupid things that I had done resulted from my becoming enraged, for no apparent good reason or over trivial matters.

For instance, I remember coming home from work one Saturday night, and I saw that no one had taken a tied-up garbage bag out to the garbage cans. That was the job of the older boys, Jerry Jr., 13, or even Christopher, 9. I pulled the bag up onto my foot platforms, and for no other reason than that the girls' room was closer to me than the bedroom occupied by the four boys, I pushed the bag of garbage off my foot platforms and then shoved it into the girls' room using the electric wheelchair's power.

As I went down the hallway to our bedroom, I could hear Michelle, then 14, saying in a frightened and puzzled voice, "Mom, why did Dad put the garbage into our room?"

Earlier in that summer of 1984, Jeannie and the kids had adopted yet another in a long line of dogs that I eventually gave away. This one was a truly ugly, scrawny dog they called "Sheba."

I loaded all my sour feelings upon that dog. One afternoon, in my electric wheelchair I chased that poor dog all over the patio, cursing and swearing at it like a lunatic.

Even when I went on outings with Jeannie and the kids to our favorite spot, Caesar's Creek Lake, I would go far away in my electric wheelchair from the family down by the lake.

If I wasn't "non-communicating" with Jeannie, I was viciously wounding her with my most savage weapon, sarcasm. There were many times when I brought tears to her eyes by saying something like, "Oh, sure, why not go to the grocery and conveniently forget your husband's favorite Stouffer dinner?"

Or, "With the way you organize things, you better start getting ready for tomorrow's noon mass at about 6 p.m. tonight."

When I spoke to Jeannie, I cut her heart. When I did not speak to Jeannie, I cut her heart.

Why she took it for so long is still a mystery to me.

My regular doctor, internist Dr. Ramesh Gandhi, prescribed limited, mild dosages of a series of tranquilizers including Elavil, Librium, and Valium. He also prescribed a mild dosage of the antidepressant Sinequan when I began psychotherapy.

The psychologist set up an appointment with the staff psychiatrist, but when I went into see him, the interview lasted no more than five minutes. "I have no idea why they sent you to me," he said. With that kind of reception, I had no idea why I should stay in his office. I left.

The first psychologist that I saw treated me with talk therapy once a week for several months. Finally, he said, "We have gone about as far as we can go together. I would like to see you go to an associate of mine who conducts biofeedback sessions. He might be able to help you more."

The second psychologist had me listen to tapes of sounds such as the movement of waves, or the soft rushing of wind. I was supposed to find a way to relax.

Unfortunately, I have a personality that runs hot and heavy all the time. On the exterior I may have seemed to be calm. On the interior, I was constantly churning and always looking for some new task to take on, or some new mountain to conquer. After nearly two months of attempts at finding some biofeedback technique that would help me to relax, the psychologist figuratively threw up his hands.

"Jerry, you are like the mythical Greek figure Sisyphus. You are determined to keep pushing your own personal boulder up a hill, and when it reaches the top and inevitably starts to roll back down the hill, you will run like hell back down the hill and start the process all over again.

"If you continue this, you will once again find yourself in mental-health counseling. There is only so much a therapist can do for you. You have to decide when it is time to stop and enjoy life."

With that, my psychological counseling came to a close. Much good had been done, but what we did not know was that we had merely scratched the surface.

At least things got better at home for Jeannie and the kids. I tried hard to eliminate the sarcasm, and I tried to take a greater interest in my children's affairs. I would use time off to make sure that I saw Mickie's soccer and softball games, Jerry Jr.'s freshman high school football games, Mary Rose's junior high soccer games, and Christopher's peewee football games.

In September 1985, Dayton Newspapers Inc. formally merged "The Journal Herald," the morning paper with the "Daily News." We became an all-morning operation. That meant that the editing crew—the news desk and the copy desk—would work at night.

My new work schedule had me working 4 p.m. to midnight on Tuesday, Wednesday, and Thursday. I continued as the designated editor on the "God squad" on Fridays working only noon to 6 p.m. On Saturdays, it was 4 p.m. to midnight.

Many people from both of the papers were unhappy with the change, but I was privately pleased because it meant that I would be able to get enough sleep, or so I hoped.

The down side was that I would be seeing less of my children.

We had a magnificent arts critic by the name of Betty Dietz Krebs. She had been at the paper for nearly five decades. She covered both the Dayton Philharmonic and the Cincinnati Symphony Orchestra. Many of the other copy editors were leery of her imperious and sharp-tongued style of dealing with editors.

Betty and I always seemed to get along. When I would see her stepping off the elevator between editions, I would call out, "Bong! Bong! Bong! Betty alert! Betty alert! This is not a drill!" The other editors would know not to pull up her story on their screens. They gladly gave the task to me.

The merger of the two newspapers created a great deal of discontent. I joined a group of people headed by reporters Rob Modic, Dave Allbaugh, Wes Hills, and copy editor Charley Stough. We believed the time was right for our in-house union to join the International Newspaper Guild. With a lot of our people being forced to work at night, and with a lot of unhappy "Journal Herald" people coming down to the third floor, things seemed right for the move.

The company offered a contract that we militants rejected out of hand. I had been on the union's negotiating committee, and I had seen the arrogance of the company executives up close. It was not a pretty sight.

It was during the three-hour debate over the contract that a mirror was held up, and I got to see myself in a way that deflated me. Young Mike Kessler had worked his way up the ladder without college training from clerk to an editor of the newspaper's weekly TV listings book. In speaking about the contract, he quite innocently gave me the worst backhanded compliment I had ever gotten.

"Look at Jerry Range," he said. "So what if his pants get wet when he goes to the men's room, and so what if he can't get the zipper back up all the away. He still gives everything he has to the job."

"Lord, save me from well-meaning people," I said to myself.

The contract passed, 58-49, much to the disappointment of those of us who were militant unionists. We naturally saw defeat looming on the issue of becoming a part of the International Newspaper Guild.

I spoke passionately against the contract, and for joining the international Guild.

After another three-hour debate on the issue of joining the Guild, there was another vote.

Inexplicably, the proposal for joining with the Guild passed by the same margin, 58-49. As time went by, more people came over to the union side. The union filed an unfair labor practice charge against the company. I was called to testify in Montgomery County Common Please Court.

When it came time for me to offer testimony, I took the oath and then said to the court's chief judge: "Your honor, may I speak of something else before the company's lawyers question me?"

"Yes, by all means," the bemused jurist said.

"Your honor, you have a government building here that is not wheelchair friendly." He was taken aback. "I tried to use a number of the men's rooms, and none was accessible. In addition, I even tried one of the women's restrooms after my wife Jeannie first made sure the coast was clear. It too was not accessible. You have some serious problems here, your honor. This directly impacts on the ability of a person in a wheelchair to get an equal chance at justice."

"Would you be willing to meet with my executive secretary?" the judge asked. I said that I would be willing to do anything to make the county courts building more accessible.

A week later I took the judge's executive secretary through all of the restrooms in the building. In one of the women's restrooms, I said, "What does a woman need in this restroom besides a toilet?" I asked.

She answered, "Why, a mirror of course."

I told her to pretend that she was sitting in a chair. She squatted down as if sitting. I said, "What do you see?"

"Nothing," she said ruefully.

"Exactly," I said, "because the mirror is placed at a level for a woman of roughly 5-foot-6 in height who is standing."

There were numerous other things such as toilet stalls blocking the entrance for a person in a wheelchair who needed the door to be fully open, sinks that were too high, doors on toilet stalls that were too narrow. There was no automatic exterior doorway to the building. They were the kinds of things that able-bodied people had no need to consider, and the kinds of things that crippled people expected.

Our backyard neighbors from 1977 when we moved into our first house were the Carters: Rick, head football coach at the University of Dayton; his wife Deanne, and their sons Nick, then about 14, and Andy, 6, Mary Rose's age.

We were not close personal friends of the Carters, but we were on friendly terms with them. In football season 1979, Carter's UD Flyers ran the table, went 14-0, and won the NCAA Division III national title in Phoenix City, Ala. We watched the game on Dayton television. While the team was flying home from Alabama, Jeannie and the kids went over to the Carter home and decorated the house with congratulatory messages and balloons.

Later that night, we watched Carter hoist the national trophy in front of a roaring crowd of UD students at the campus fieldhouse. By then it was almost 11 p.m. An hour later Jeannie and I were in the family room. There was a rap on our patio door. A thick curtain covered it.

"Who could that be?" she said. "Should I call the police?"

"Let's take a look," I said. Standing outside on our patio was Carter. Jeannie opened the door, and the diminutive coach stepped in.

"I just wanted to say how much I appreciate what you folks did," he said, "it really means a lot." We congratulated him again, and he left.

"There goes a class act," I said to Jeannie.

Indeed, he was on his way to classier things. Holy Cross College in Worcester, Mass., was looking to upgrade its football program. Holy Cross got wind of a successful young coach at the Catholic University of Dayton. Holy Cross wanted Carter.

Besides a healthy increase in pay, Holy Cross promised Carter that the school would build new locker rooms and add an improved weight room. In 1980, Carter's first Holy Cross team became the first team there to have a winning season in 20 years.

After that, Holy Cross alumni revered Carter, as he posted 9-2, or 10-1 seasons year after year. However, in 1985 he had his first losing season, 4-6-1, as a head coach at four different schools: two small colleges in Indiana, the University of Dayton, and Holy Cross.

His father, with whom he was very close, died unexpectedly in the fall of 1985. At the very end of the year, his mother died of cancer. In addition, Holy Cross announced that it was dropping football scholarships. Carter saw that as a betrayal of what he had been told six years before. He had just begun treatment for clinical depression.

In February 1986 about 2 a.m., I was sitting at the kitchen table reading a book after work. I had the sports network ESPN on in the background with the sound turned down. Out of the corner of my eye, I saw Carter's picture.

I said to myself, "Great! Rick got that big job that he always wanted in the Midwest at a Big Ten school."

I grabbed the clicker, and turned up the volume in time to hear the announcer say, " . . . was found today by his son Nick hanged in their Worcester, Mass., home."

Our paper had a weeklong series of stories on Carter with testimonials from many of his former players and from others in the community. I asked our managing editor, Joe Fenley, if I could write a short piece on the possible state of Carter's mind when he took his life.

I wrote in part: "Some people reach a point in their lives when they are required to climb through a window. Some make it through, as I recently did. Others do not. Rick Carter did not make it through that window. We should think no less of him as a man because of that."

Fenley read the story on his VDT, came out to me and said, "Jerry, are you sure that you want to say this, I mean, indicating that you have had your own mental and emotional difficulties?"

"Absolutely, Joe," I said. "I'm not ashamed of being treated for depression, and if it helps someone else who is depressed to get treatment, then we will have accomplished something."

The story ran prominently in the first page of the sports section. I was enormously gratified to get a note from Carter's widow, Deanne, in which she graciously thanked me for the piece.

It was not too long after Carter's death that cracks began to appear in the wallpapering that the psychologists had done on my psyche.

By early 1988, the black beast was reappearing from his hidden lair deep down in my heart. (We have since learned that he will always be there, lurking, waiting for an opportunity to strike). Again, I began to talk less and less about anything of substance to Jeannie. And I no longer was making totally rational decisions.

Mary Rose, then a seventh grader, was walking with her friend Amanda Muzechuk near the Muzechuk home when they saw a "For Sale" sign on the lawn of a ranch-type home just behind Alter High School and St. Charles School. There was an open house.

The two young girls were bold as brass. They gave the house a thorough look-see. Mary Rose came home that evening and said, "Daddy, will you come and take a look at the house for sale on Pepper Hill?"

For several days, I held out against Mary Rose's pleas. Only a month before, a benefactor with a heart larger than all of Dayton had given us $41,000. The benefactor knew how much our debts weighed upon us. For the first time in our married lives, we were free of debt.

I did not want to take on a responsibility like a larger mortgage that would get us back into financial difficulty. But seventh-grade girls have a way of working on you, and Mary Rose was nothing if not persistent.

Finally, I agreed to look. Obviously, the location was great. Our kids would be able to walk to school, and we all would be able to walk (or roll) to church. The house was on a cul-de-sac, and the kids could slip through a gate in the fence separating the schools' playing fields from the neighborhood. Jeannie loved the location.

"You will be able to roll for a long way on sidewalks in the electric," she said. "That might help you feel better—to get out on your own," she added. "And," she said in the clincher, "you'll be able to see freshmen and reserve football games on Alter's football field."

We both had seen the signs of depression coming like a train gathering speed on a downhill track. This time it was not so much that I was wound up tightly inside. This time, there simply was no fuel left in my emotional tank. The union battle, the long lonely nights at work, and my continuing sense of under-achievement took their toll.

The vicious and voracious beast of depression wraps itself around a person's heart and shuts out all the sunshine.

Three months after we occupied the new house, Jeannie and I sat at the kitchen table after all the kids were asleep. Once again she was asking me to get professional help. This time, we were members of an HMO called Western Ohio. It recommended that we seek counseling at what was called Metropolitan Clinic of Counseling.

We called. We were told that first a staff psychiatrist would interview me, and possibly prescribe medication. The psychiatrist would be working together on my case with a psychologist. So we made the appointment, and awaited my first session with the psychiatrist, Dr. Toni Carmen.

Her first question was, "Are you sleeping very well?"

"Well, I have not been a good sleeper since age 11 when I got polio. But lately getting to sleep has been almost impossible, and when I do sleep, I only sleep for a few hours," I said.

She said, "The first thing I am going to do is to give you Dr. Carmen's prescription for sleep. Do know what chamomile tea is?"

"Sure, Winnie the Pooh drank it," I said.

"I want you to take a cup of chamomile tea every night about an hour before you want to go to sleep and put a large spoonful of honey in it. Then I want you to take four amino acid tablets. They will trigger a reaction in your brain that will cause your brain to order your body to flood itself with endorphins, which are natural relaxants."

I always have followed doctors' orders to the letter, so I did as the psychiatrist ordered and took the maximum dosage every night as she had prescribed. Immediately, I began to sleep regularly and deeply—almost two deeply.

End of Chapter 11

CHAPTER 12

"Your Husband Is Dying"

It was great to be able to sleep again.

Meanwhile, I began psychoanalysis with a lady by the name of Louise.

I had no trouble bearing my heart and soul to this kindly middle-aged woman with a warm smile and a soft voice.

We covered the entire gamut of my life and times since age 11. I began by telling her of the first night that I spent in the hospital back in Erie, Pa.

"I remember seeing the streetlights go on. I guess it must have been around 8:30, because it was the middle of August. I remember watching Peach Street and the few cars that moved under those lights throughout the night. Finally, I remember those streetlights reluctantly flickering out as the sky got lighter in the east."

"And I remember thinking to myself, 'Gee, I have never stayed up all night before'," I said.

We delved deeply into the effects of the long separations from my family, the long distance from home when I went to college, and the compressed time from when I was crippled until I began my work life in Cleveland. I tried to describe for her the effect that Metcalf and other oddballs at the "Plain Dealer" had on me.

We talked about expectations that my parents had for me, and the expectations that I had put on myself. Deeper and deeper, Louise had me crawl down into my subconscious.

Finally after the psychoanalytic sessions had stretched about four months, I said to her, "There is something than I haven't revealed, because I'm rather embarrassed by it."

"Do you feel comfortable talking about it now?" she asked.

"Comfortable? No, but I feel that I have to do it now," I said.

I began then to tell her the Jacque story. I told her of how I believed it had been more than a teenage crush. I said there was real love involved back then in the early '60s. I told her how there was almost no physical interaction between us.

I rarely had thought of her over a 20-year span of time.

"And then," I said, "when my world started to go to hell in the early 1980s, the memory of her showed up like an uninvited relative asking for a place to stay."

"Why are you so angry about the memories?" she asked.

"Well, first of all, I have been married to a beautiful woman for 20 years. Second, we have six children. Third, I am in love with my wife Jeannie."

"And No. 4, Jacque hurt me badly and left me bleeding badly."

Louise: "Be more specific, what did she do that so bothers you?"

"Well, first, she cut off our relationship like a butcher chops a piece of meat in half," I said. "Why did it have to be so brutal?"

"We never spoke again. This is 1989, and that makes 27 years.

"But what really angers me is the fact that after all these years it still bothers me. It is like an old wound that rips open long after the doctor and the patient believed it was healed."

"What do we do to end this odd hemorrhage?" Louise asked.

We talked about it, and Louise suggested that I write Jacque a letter. I agreed to do it.

A reporter friend of mine in Pittsburgh tracked her down, verified that she was indeed the Jacque who had once removed me from her life. She had long since left the convent.

I wrote a letter to her that essentially boiled down to three questions. First, I asked her that when we were teenagers, did she have no emotional attachment to me?

Second, I asked why she had so coldly ended our high school "romance."

Third, I asked why had she never acknowledged my existence after high school?

She eventually wrote me in care of the "Daily News."

As to emotional attachment, she said, "I was aware we were an 'item' in high school, but you put much more into it than I did. I never regarded us as more than 'good friends.'"

On the meat-cleaver cut-off, she simply said that was for the best.

She did not say why she never acknowledged my existence years later.

A few days later I went to Jeannie and said we needed to talk. We went over to the high school and she sat under a tree. I showed Jeannie the letter that I had gotten from Jacque.

Jeannie's reaction surprised me: "You mean you put that poor woman through that emotional ringer? Come on, we're going home!"

When we got home, Jeannie called Jacque in Pittsburgh. From what I could hear, my wife and my high school girlfriend had a pleasant 20-minute chat. When Jeannie told her that we had six children, Jacque's reply was, "He wouldn't have gotten six children out of me."

By now it was May.

Incrementally, my functioning ability had been decreasing, but it was so slow in happening that I really did not recognize anything was happening to my body until at least six months had gone by.

It was becoming increasingly difficult for me to function in the men's room. Again, the changes were so imperceptible that it was not until late April or early May that I realized something was wrong. I was having trouble reaching down to unlock my footrests, and to lock the brakes so that I could stay in place at the wall urinal.

By early May I could barely zip my pants. In late May on two consecutive nights I flooded my pants in the men's room. Each time, I had to tell someone who came into the men's room to call my home and to tell my wife to come and get me.

I gave news editor Beyer a memo explaining that something had happened to my body that made it impossible for me to function in the newsroom. I was called to a meeting with Ann Pettee, chief of the copy desk; Beyer, and Ken Canfield, assistant news editor. We huddled together at one corner of the huge table in the "Governor's Library," which had been used for daily meetings since the time of former Ohio Gov. James Cox, founder of the Cox newspaper chain.

I began to tell them of my difficulties, and said that Jeannie and I thought that possibly I had been hit by post-polio syndrome, which had been occurring in small numbers among the fewer than 300,000 former polio patients still alive in the United States.

Then I began to cry. After an awkward period of time, to my astonishment the three of them suggested that I might be able to continue to work at home.

"The technology is evolving rapidly and on the market now is equipment that can connect you at home with us here in the newsroom," Ann said. "It may take time to get it, but we're willing to try if you are."

"Yeah," Beyer said, "if I were you, I wouldn't go home today and wait by the phone. But eventually we'll be calling you."

Ann said that K.J. Peterson, who often filled in as copy desk chief, would be working with me at my home when the equipment was located and purchased. Peterson, an emigre from Minnesota, had immersed himself in the mysteries of newspaper computerology.

Peterson was a loner and a man of few words. He was, however, a good guy who had introduced me to what became one of my favorite movies, "Tender Mercies." Down through the years, that movie has been a useful emotional tool for me.

I was not pleased with what was happening to my body over the summer and early fall months of 1989. I was less and less able to care for myself. By October, I could no longer pick up a cup of coffee. Jeannie had taken a job at a Catholic nursing home. She would leave me at the table in the kitchen with a book in front of me and with the TV clicker nearby on the tabletop. When she returned from work eight hours later, she would find me slumped over the table asleep.

One day in late November I awoke and called out to her in anguish: "I have a stabbing pain in my left thumb. Oh, my God, it hurts! It hurts!"

Someone somewhere had a voodoo doll marked "Jerry Range" and was stabbing the doll's left thumb with a huge sharp needle.

"I'll call Dr. Keyes for some kind of pain medication," Jeannie said.

"This is going to sound ridiculous, you telling them that I have a pain in my thumb." But the pain was so sharp and so intense that I did not argue. Pain was also beginning in my right thumb.

Dr. Keyes gave me a pain prescription. The initial dosage gave only an hour or two of relief. We were allowed to increase the dosage to the point where I could get three to four hours of relief.

In a few weeks, the pain switched to my feet. Dr. Keyes tried a brief regimen of steroid medication. It did not help much.

I took the amino acid tablets up through October. By then, my sessions with Louise had ended, and my periodic meetings with Dr. Carmen also had ended.

Once again, I had beaten back the beast of depression. The irony was that the real battle was about to begin.

An odd event intruded during our descent toward oblivion. Early in October, I got a call from Joe Konitzky, assistant director of the Rehab Center at the University of Illinois.

"Jerry, at our annual Rehab Center banquet at Homecoming time we want to present you with the Harold Scharper Award for lifetime achievement," my old friend said.

"Good Lord, Joe, you guys are really scraping the bottom of the barrel," I said. "There must be other people who are far more deserving then I am. What have I done to deserve such an honor?"

(The late Harold Scharper was one of the original five veterans of World War II who Dr. Nugent had used to begin his Rehab Center).

"Jerry," Konitzky said, "you are the guy we want. Will you accept?"

I could never refuse a request from that wonderful man, Joe Konitzky. "Yes, Joe, I would be pleased to accept."

Someone at the local CBS affiliate in Dayton, WHIO, got wind of the award. A reporter and a cameraman came to the house and interviewed me with Jeannie and all the children around me. The station arranged for a satellite feed by its affiliate in Champaign-Urbana.

During my acceptance speech, I told the story about Dr. Nugent using reverse psychology to keep me at the University of Illinois. In retelling the story, I said, "Dr. Nugent said, 'Go ahead and leave, you sniveling little son of a bitch!'"

After the formal ceremonies, Dr. Nugent, now retired, came up to me and said with some real pain in his eyes and in his voice, "Jerry, I didn't really call you a son of a bitch, did I?"

I paused in my reply for half a heartbeat, and then said, "No, Tim, I just used poetic license to get a good laugh."

As the blazing colors of fall faded into the stale gray of the oncoming Ohio winter, I was approaching physical helplessness. Jeannie had to drag me out of bed, feed me, wash me, get me on and off the toilet. I was of little use with the kids.

Dr. Keyes sent us to a neurosurgeon who told us bluntly, "There's nothing I can do for you." Keyes also sent us to a neurologist who promptly declared that I was a victim of Guillain-Barre syndrome. It is a polio-like illness that generally leaves its victims with some functioning ability.

"In your case," the neurologist said, "since you had very little muscle function left, you now have lost almost all of that functioning ability. There is no doubt that it is Guillain-Barre syndrome."

Like some other doctors, he reached a conclusion and was backtracking for symptoms to prove it. He was a pompous ass.

In early December, we went to Dr. David Johnson, the head of the rehabilitation unit at what was then St. Elizabeth Hospital, near downtown Dayton. Dr. Johnson examined me thoroughly, took some blood tests, did some other testing and said, "I really do not know what your problem is. I wish I could tell you for sure, but I cannot."

That is the kind of honesty a patient appreciates. Dr. Johnson did begin a regimen of traction on me while I was sitting in my wheelchair. The plan was to do it Monday, Wednesday, and Friday. Unfortunately, almost immediately after the traction was started at each session, I would fall soundly asleep.

After three or four sessions of my sleeping in the wheelchair with my head held straight by the combinations of weights and pulleys, Dr. Johnson ended that treatment. It was getting close to Christmas. I was beginning to drift away from time and reality.

On each of three successive days, I sat on the raised commode at home and had trouble breathing. I did not tell Jeannie about it. For some reason, I was unable to put two and two together and come up with the conclusion that something was terribly wrong.

On Dec. 20, 1989, I awoke with an ache across my chest. Jeannie pulled me out of bed and got me into the wheelchair. She started pushing me down the hallway. I suddenly doubled over and was gasping for breath.

It was at that point that one of those surreal moments in life occurred; the point at which a crisis arises, but practicality still is in place.

"Call 911," I said to Jeannie as I was gasping for air.

"But if I call 911, the emergency crew will take you to Kettering Memorial Hospital, and I want you to go to a Catholic hospital. I want them to take you to St. E's."

Gasping for air, I managed to say, "Sweetheart (gasp!), if you don't do something soon (gasp!), it won't make any difference where I go (gasp!), because I cannot breathe."

"I will drive you to St. E's myself," she said.

"Just do it soon," I gasped again.

We arrived at St. E's around noon. I spent 7 1/2 hours in the emergency room.

Our primary care physician, Dr. Keyes, ordered breathing treatments. I was so disoriented that I yelled at Jeannie.

"Get my goddam shoes and socks out of the closet, and take me home. I'm just fine (gasp!)."

Jeannie convinced me that I needed to stay in the hospital "a little bit longer."

I was there 60 days.

On the second night of my hospitalization, Jeannie was in the chapel meditating and praying. She was startled when Dr. Carmen slipped into the pew next to Jeannie. Dr. Carmen asked her, "Have any of the doctors who were on Jerry's case linked his problems with any of his medications?"

"No, I don't think so," Jeannie said.

"Good," the psychiatrist said.

"I am sure he will be okay," she said as she took her leave.

On the third night, about 4 a.m., a nurse told Jeannie, "They're not doing enough. Your husband is dying, and no one seems to be interested. Call Dr. Keyes."

"You mean call Dr. Keyes right now at 4 a.m.—it's that bad?"

"Yes," the nurse said.

So Jeannie immediately called Dr. Keyes. Dr. Keyes immediately ordered me sent to the cardiac intensive care unit. Soon after that, I was sent to the so-called "step-down unit" in the game of spin the dying patient.

The nurses told Jeannie she could not stay overnight in my room. When she came back early in the morning, she learned that I had almost choked to death on my own saliva. By then, I could not even lift my head off the pillow.

The nursing staff relented, and Jeannie was allowed to stay overnight. She was not allowed to sleep in the other hospital bed in the semi-private room. So during her first night, she slept on the floor. On the second night, some kind soul located a gurney for her to use as a bed.

I was still hallucinating. My breathing was becoming more labored even with the help of a respiratory tube put down through my nasal passages into the lung. There was also a feeding tube stuck through my mouth down into my stomach.

At this point, the fifth doctor to take an interest in the case was Dr. Eduardo Casalmir, a gentle and caring man. Of the five doctors involved in the case, Dr. Casalmir was the only one to see that my diaphragm was not functioning properly.

Basically on my case I had three blind mice, a good guy who was out of his realm of expertise, which was rehabilitation, and a caring pulmonary specialist.

He told Jeannie, "If your husband does not have a tracheotomy, he will surely die—soon."

"Then do the tracheotomy as soon as you can," Jeannie replied.

After the tracheotomy surgery and in my second day as a full-fledged member of the intensive care club, Jeannie came into my cubicle to see me being given a pint of blood intravenously.

"Who ordered this?" she demanded of the nurse on duty.

"Last night your husband's blood pressure went dangerously low," the nurse responded. "So the neurologist ordered blood given."

The day after I had my tracheotomy surgery, the neurologist ordered a lumbar puncture in which fluid is drawn from the spinal column while the patient is awake. The word "torture" best applies. The technicians flipped me over, forcing the tracheotomy tube into my throat. Luckily, one of the young nurses on my floor had accompanied me. She quickly got a pillow under my chest. That relieved the pressure on my throat.

The head nurse asked Jeannie if she wanted a "code" called if a major event occurred to me such as a heart attack. In other words, did Jeannie want them to use extraordinary means to keep me alive.

"Jerry would not want to live when he did not have his mental capacities intact," Jeannie said. So she signed the form absolving hospital personnel from responsibility to take extraordinary means to keep me alive.

It was Christmastime. Jeannie had a husband slipping away in the hospital. She had a kindergartener and a second grader at home. Our oldest child, Mickie, 18, was performing heroic duty taking care of the other children, Jerry Jr., 17; Mary Rose, 15; Christopher, 13; Peter, 8, and Patrick, 5. Jeannie told Mickie that she wanted to keep everything as normal as possible.

One night she rushed home from the hospital to help with

the kids and get something to eat before going back to be with me. When she came in the front door, there was a decorated Christmas tree in the corner of the living room. She put her hands to her face, slumped wearily against the wall, and softly wept.

Mickie had come to visit me earlier. When she saw the tubes running in and out of me, she backed out into the hospital hall and began to sob hysterically.

"Why does it have to be this way? Why does Daddy have to suffer like this? Why does Daddy always have to have pain?"

My hallucinations lasted for about three weeks. The nurses had given Jeannie a board with big letters on it. By nodding my head in the direction of the letter, we were able to communicate, albeit crudely. One night when she came in, I indicated I wanted her to hold up the letter board.

She did so, and I laboriously spelled out the message, "How are the kids?"

"They are fine, and they miss you," she said.

"What did you do with them when the atomic bomb hit Dayton?" I spelled out.

The pressure affected the small children as well as the older ones. Peter was 8 at the time. His birthday was Dec. 22, two days after I went into the hospital. We celebrated his birthday in my hospital room.

Little blond-haired Peter had his hand on one of my useless legs as he stood near the bottom of the bed. His birthday cake sat on my rolling hospital tray. There were gifts waiting for him on the tray.

There were parallel lines of tears flowing down both of his cheeks.

Soon after that, Jeannie brought in seven magnetic hearts and attached them to my nightstand in a show of solidarity between her, the six children, and me.

With the "trache" in my throat connected to the ventilator, I was getting the necessary amount of oxygen. Ever so gradually, I was easing back into reality. At first the nurses tried to "wean" me off the ventilator. The first time that they did it, I "crashed" in just seconds; that is, I began to choke for lack of oxygen.

After about three weeks in intensive care, I was moved into the "step-down" unit for the second time.

That seemed to mark the solid turning point upward in the agonizing march through our family's personal hell. Luckily, I was thinking rationally again.

In rehab, the nurses concentrated on teaching Jeannie how to keep the trache clean. Then I was given a "fenestrated" trache, one which allowed me to speak in brief bursts of words. I felt as if the wall between my wife and me had been torn down.

Finally, I could tell her how anxious I got when she left the room to go home for a brief period, and how relieved I felt when she re-entered my world.

Now I could tell Jeannie how much I loved her and now much she meant to me.

The technicians assigned to the rehab unit modified my wheelchair so that the ventilator later could be carried on the back of the wheelchair. A hospital bed was set up in our living room. We were working against the clock, because my hospitalization insurance only paid for one month in rehabilitation.

Near the end of that time, I went home for a "test" of Jeannie's ability to take care of me at home and also for my ability to exist beyond the walls of the hospital. We passed our test.

On my final day in the rehab unit, three nurses visited with Jeannie and me. Speaking for all three, one said something that stunned us.

"There will come a time when you'll hate each other," she said. "It is inevitable, it always happens, and you must be ready to deal with it."

Both of us protested.

"That won't happen to us," Jeannie said.

"No way will that happen in our case," I said. "You guys must be crazy."

"Just be ready," the nurse said.

Jeannie and I were watching Headline News on CNN about

three weeks after I was discharged from the hospital. There was tape of the U.S. Surgeon General, who was saying that all amino acid tablets had been ordered removed from the shelves of American pharmacies and health food stores.

We looked at one another in stunned silence for about ten seconds. "Jerry, you took that stuff for nearly a year," Jeannie said.

"Yeah, and we were trying so many different medications that there was no reason to guess which one of them might have had an affect on me," I said.

My mother sent us a newspaper clipping. It was an Associated Press story describing the symptoms of EMS (eosynophilia myalgia syndrome).

"Jerry, you had all of these symptoms," Jeannie said.

"The first day in the hospital you had a light lemon-colored, dimpled rash on your back. I thought at the time, 'How could he develop a pressure sore in such a short time?' You had those sharp pains in your thumbs and feet. You had white stools when I took you off the bedpan—a sure sign of liver difficulty and trouble with your white blood cell count. Your stomach had swollen from 38 inches to 48 inches. You lost most of your hair."

At last there was a huge light at the end of the tunnel. We were a long way from acting on the information. The news stories ended the mystery. They made some sense out of the chaos of the previous 16 months. For the moment, that was comfort enough.

End of Chapter 12

CHAPTER 13

"You Don't Like It Here, Do You?"

Like the old joke, the bright light at the end of the tunnel was on the front of a powerful locomotive heading straight at us. The news from the U.S. Surgeon General had lifted our spirits, but more practical matters were bearing down upon us.

Immediately after coming home from the hospital, I found myself trying to keep a family that had been traumatized from spinning out of control.

I learned that Jerry Jr., then 17 and a senior in high school, had been staying out very late on school nights while I was fighting to stay alive and while Jeannie was spending most of her time at my hospital bedside. There was nothing that his older sister Mickie could do but plead with him or yell at him. He was 17, and weighed 211 pounds.

I quickly put a severe crimp in his extra-hours social life.

I set up shop in the living room. It rapidly became apparent that Jeannie would not be able to give me around-the-clock nursing care. Our insurance plan paid for eight hours of nursing service a day in the home. Luckily, Jeannie and I had veto power and were allowed to request another nurse if one proved unsatisfactory. We rejected four nurses before we finally hit the jackpot.

One was so incredibly polite that she was transparently manipulative, and we believed that she was picking up loose change. Besides, she smoked. Another had dirty fingernails. And she got her rides from young men whom we did not want anywhere near our house. A third did virtually no work, forcing Jeannie to do the job. The fourth was an elderly woman who did little more than talk of her glory days as full-time nurse to the rich widow Virginia Kettering.

Then Faye showed up. Our first impression was, "Oh, my God, not another loser!" She was from eastern Kentucky, about our age. She sounded like a hayseed. But she treated her patients with dignity. She was kind, considerate, and enormously patient.

She had no preconceived notions about how the in-home patient should be treated, other than with dignity and decency. She was a stickler for cleanliness. That was extremely important for me, because I still had the trache in my throat. Tracheotomy patients are easy and common targets for upper respiratory germs. Fortunately, I escaped pneumonia, and bronchitis, both of which were common for people with tracheotomies.

Faye showed some of the older children how to suction out the trache tube. It was constantly filling up with mucous.

She was gentle.

She waited for the patient to suggest ways of doing things. She eventually became like a member of our family.

She had been married several times. Her first marriage was basically an effort to get out of the little town where she grew up. There was a second failed marriage. She had a daughter about the age of our Mickie. Apparently my formal education impressed her so much that she sought my advice.

She told us of a man whom she had been dating. "He only seems interested in himself, and can't give much of himself to others."

"Why does she continue to date this guy?" I wondered. His name was Orval. After she had been working at our house for almost three months, she told Jeannie a secret.

Jeannie urged her to tell me. Faye came to my bedside looking frightened, and said, "I've agreed to marry Orval. I hope y'all don't think bad of me because of it." She was twisting her hands together nervously and seemed genuinely worried about my reaction.

"Faye, I would never criticize your personal choices. Who am I to judge you or anyone else? Jeannie and I only want the best for you, because you were so kind to us when we really needed someone with nursing expertise, someone we could trust, so that Jeannie could get some much-needed rest.

"You have been that person, and then some. We wish you nothing but happiness in your coming marriage."

She stood at the foot of my bed in the living room and gently cried. I still do not understand why she felt that she needed my approval.

It wasn't as if we were the Partridge family.

Late on a bitterly cold Friday night in March, Jeannie answered the phone and uttered a quick painful, "Oh!"

"I will be right there," she said and hung up the phone.

"The police are holding Jerry Jr. down at the grocery store," she said. "He tried to shoplift some things." She hurriedly threw on her coat, checked my trache and the ventilator. Then she hurried out the door.

The chill inside me matched the weather outside. When she got back with Jerry Jr., Jeannie came over to my bed. "The police agreed not to arrest him after the store manager heard our story and said that he would not press charges. Would you talk to him? I am simply worn out." She then went to the back of the house and lay down.

Jerry Jr. was in the kitchen. I called him to my bedside. "I'm not going to yell at you or lecture you," I said.

"Now is not the time for that. Besides, I can't yell very good with this trache in my throat. This is what I want you to do. It is about 20 degrees outside. Take a long walk, breathe the cold night air deeply, and think about what you did. When you've thought it through, come back and we'll talk."

He was gone for about half an hour. When he came back into the house, he rushed to my bedside and wrapped his arms around me. He began to sob uncontrollably. He said, "I didn't do it to hurt you, Dad. I didn't do it to hurt you, I didn't do it to hurt you!"

He had shoplifted suntan lotion and a cheap pair of sunglasses from a store that had hired him to work after he returned from a spring break vacation in Florida. The amount for the items he took was about $10. He had more than enough in his wallet to pay for it.

"Why did you do it, Jerry?"

"I don't know, I just don't know. I picked out the two items and stuck them in my pocket and started to walk out of the store," he said. "Then the manager told me to wait while he called the police. All I could think of was, 'What am I going to say to Dad?'"

I allowed him to go to Florida. He would be under the supervision of adults we trusted. He knew he had done wrong. He knew he had done a stupid thing. Any punishment by me couldn't be as bad as the emotional beating up he had inflicted on himself.

Later, he would work his way through college as a store detective for JC Penney. At a Penney store in New Philadelphia, he wrestled with a shoplifter who escaped with several pairs of denim jeans after he sucker-punched Jerry. While attending the University of Cincinnati full-time, he worked as a store detective at a Penney outlet.

He graduated with a degree in criminal justice, and married a fiery-red-haired department head in that store. Her name was Karen, and their marriage has been an enriching experience for both of them, and for the rest of us.

For about two months, we anxiously waited the installation of the computer that the company had promised. It arrived toward the end of April. Peterson, my designated computer guru, came to the house a number of times.

The computer sat a few feet from my hospital bed. Peter, then a second-grader, typed for me. I began to edit two or three stories a night.

Ann Pettee told me over the phone, "Ken Canfield is redesigning Page 2. We want to spice it up with short, light-hearted stories, as well as running the weather forecast and the almanac there. You'll have a daily opportunity to display your specialty—writing those poetic cutlines that everyone likes."

By now it was June 12. "The makeover of Page 2 will probably start at the beginning of July," Ann said.

"Hey, I will be a page editor," I said. "I'm really looking forward to getting started on this."

Later the same day, the managing editor's secretary called to ask if I could come for a meeting the next day at 2 p.m.

"Well, a trip outside the house will be a good test for us," I said. We had a 1986 Ford van equipped with a hydraulic lift for the wheelchair. I told her we could be there at 2 p.m.

Soon after her call, I got a call from Rob Modic, union president. He said, "Jerry, I just heard about the meeting. I'm sorry to be the one to tell you, but this is no ordinary meeting to check on your progress. Sidlo (managing editor), will tell you that you're being fired. Technically, they're putting you on disability retirement, but really, it's a firing."

"After all the hell that we have been through the past 19 months, after all of Jeannie's worrying, praying her way through gut-wrenching crisis after gut-wrenching crisis, and after our lives have been turned upside down—after all that, you're saying they're going to can me? Jesus, Rob, they sure have a long memories, don't they?"

I was referring to my part in the group that had campaigned vigorously for affiliation with the International Newspaper Guild. I was not a key player in that effort, but I tried hard to convince other staffers that it was the right thing to do. I made no secret of my convictions as I campaigned for the union's affiliation with the International Guild.

I was proud of my limited efforts to join with those people of courage who wanted to bring a real union to a group of people who were proud of their efforts to produce a good paper. Many of those hard workers were mistreated, and deserved far better.

"Jerry," Modic said, "do you want me to attend the meeting with you and Jeannie?"

"Yeah, Rob, I think we can use a friend in there. I would appreciate it if you came in with us."

The next day I went through the newsroom with the trache in

my throat. The few staff people who were there greeted me warmly. Then Jeannie, Modic, a few other union people, and I went into Sidlo's office.

I was interested to see that Madolyn Mumma, the director of human resources, and some of her subordinates were waiting along with Sidlo, and Canfield, the news editor.

As everyone else took a seat, I said to myself, "Who thinks up these oxymoronic euphemisms like 'human resources'?"

Sidlo, who was about 6-foot-2, stood up and began to speak. Able-bodied people think that towering over a cripple gives them an advantage in discourse. What it really does is anger cripples like me.

Sidlo spoke as if he had memorized lines from a script. The body language of Mumma, the "human resources" person, told me who was really in charge.

Sidlo said, "You must give us 40 hours of work a week by June 30, or we will have to place you on disability retirement."

"Steve," I said, "if you would talk to your news editor, you would learn that I have not worked a 40-hour week for more than 12 years. In fact, it was often a 32-hour week."

Sidlo was taken aback. He stumbled around for words and then finally said, "Well, nevertheless, you must give us a 40-hour workweek by June 30."

"Hell, Steve," I said, "you might as well ask me to climb Mount Everest by June 30. Is this what I get for 17 years of quality work? I'll be able to steadily increase my work time, but it might be six months or more before I can give you that 40-hour week."

Sidlo was adamant about the June 30 deadline.

Modic spoke up.

"Steve, can you give Jerry a letter stating that if a doctor signs off on him working 40 hours a week, you will promise that he can have his job back?"

Sidlo glanced at the "human resources" director, got a barely perceptible nod, and said, "Yes, I can do that."

I have often thought about exercising my option just to get their panicked reaction.

The meeting broke up. There were no parting pleasantries. As the elevator door closed on the newsroom, I watched 17 years of my life fade away.

Under the company's forced retirement plan, I would get 90 percent of my previous year's salary for six months. Then, I would get 60 percent of the average of the previous five years' salaries. Roughly, my income would drop from just under $40,000 a year to about $21,000 a year. Most of that would be in Social Security payments.

We were paying out nearly $1,000 on first and second mortgages. In addition, four children were still in Catholic schools. We considered Catholic education crucial for our children.

We were still paying on the wheelchair van. There were medical bills yet to be paid. I assumed that we could stay in the Dayton area, but I saw no way that we could keep the house. It was either sell it, or lose it. It was unlikely we could stay in the St. Charles and Alter districts.

I called my brother Tom, who lived in Dover, Ohio. Dover was the "sister" city to New Philadelphia, the county seat of Tuscarawas County, Ohio's most unspellable and most unpronounceable county.

I often had jokingly accused Tom of being the slum landlord king of Dover-New Philadelphia. He owned about seven rental properties. He sold lasers to the construction industry. He used the rental properties for tax shelters.

He said that a property in New Philadelphia was coming open, and I could rent it for slightly less than $400 a month. New Philadelphia is a small city of only 17,000 people. The house was midway (about a mile) between Sacred Heart Church and little Tuscarawas Central Catholic High School. I promised him an answer by the 4th of July.

If we could have found a comparable house in the southern suburbs of Dayton, we would be looking at rent of at least $800. It was now clear that the bright light that we had seen at the end of the tunnel was on the front of one hell of a big train.

As she had done in the past few years, Mary Rose, who was to be a sophomore at Alter High School in the fall, was vacationing with her best friend, Colleen, and her family on the Jersey shore. Alter's athletic department had paid $120 each for Mary Rose and three other Alter students to attend a football trainer's clinic.

I called my old mentor and longtime friend, Coach Art Teynor, football coach at Tuscarawas Central Catholic. I explained our situation and asked him if he could take on Mary Rose as a team trainer.

"As a matter of fact," he said, "our first girl trainer just graduated. I would love to have your Mary Rose, but she has to understand that at a small school like this she will be doing much more than just taping ankles and helping with minor injuries. She will have to wash uniforms, keep the locker room cleaned up and do other things that trainers at a school the size of Alter would never have to do."

I thanked the old coach. I told him that I would get back to him.

The July 4th holiday weekend arrived. It was decision time. If we stayed, we would surely lose the house. If we went, it meant more trauma for an already traumatized bunch of children. As Jeannie and the children slept in the back of the house, I sat in shadows in the living room with my throat connected to the ventilator. We had 17 years of roots planted in the Dayton area. I was agonizing over the decision.

Only a short time before, we had assumed that we would spend the rest of our lives in Dayton. "Should I pull up the roots," I asked myself, "or should I settle for something in Dayton that will not please anyone in the family?"

It seemed a lose/lose situation. In the wee hours of the 4th of July, I decided that we would move 200 miles northeast. Later that day I called my brother and told him I wanted to rent the house. Next, I called the Coach and told him that I would offer the trainer's job to Mary Rose when she returned.

A week later Mary Rose came skipping into the living room late at night after her vacation on the New Jersey shore. We had not been talking much for more than a month before she left. Now she jumped up onto my bed and faced me as I sat in the wheelchair. For 20 minutes, she chattered on, telling me about all the fun things that they had done, and the wondrous things they had seen.

As she was bubbling over, I said to myself, "This is the first real conversation we have had in over a month, and in a few minutes, I'm going to have to destroy her world."

Finally she paused in her narrative.

"Mary Rose," I said, "I'm glad that you had a great time with Colleen and her family on the Jersey shore, but now I have to tell you that we must move out of Kettering to live in New Philadelphia."

Her face turned gray. Her hand went to her mouth. She jumped off the bed and ran to the bathroom. She did not say a word to me for an entire week. Finally, I had to tell her about Coach Teynor's offer.

"If you want to do it, I must know in one week," I said to the sullen young woman.

Next, I called Sacred Heart School in New Philadelphia, and talked to the principal, Diane Perry. I explained our traumatic situation.

"We will welcome all of your children, Mr. Range," she said.

"Should I talk to the pastor about the tuition problem?" I asked.

"Mr. Range," she said, "your plate is already overflowing with problems. Let me take care of this one for you—the 'tuition problem,' as you put it. Believe me, Mr. Range, we do not see it as a problem. Let's enroll the kids and worry about the money later."

Mary Rose came to me and said in a defeated monotone that she would take on the trainer's job at Tuscarawas Central Catholic.

High school football preseason began early in August, as did junior high school preseason. Both she and Christopher would have to go up to New Philadelphia about three weeks before the rest of us did.

Christopher was an eighth-grader and was eligible to play for the Dover St. Joe team that welcomed players from Sacred Heart as well as players from Dennison St. Mary's at the southern end of the county. The team served as a "feeder" squad for the varsity

Saints of Tuscarawas Central Catholic. They stayed with their Uncle Jim and his wife Peg, who lived within sight of Central.

Before we left Dayton, staff members at the "Daily News" did an unbelievably generous thing. At least 60 or 70 staff members signed up to have money taken from their weekly paychecks at the credit union located in the "Daily News" building. For nearly a year, Jeannie and I received a weekly check from those big-hearted people.

On our final weekend, a group of people made up of former "Journal Herald" staffers and staff people from the old "Daily News" gave us a picnic. It was a bittersweet event. Truly, I never knew that so many people cared so much about the staff cripple.

I tried not to be bitter with specific management people at the "Daily News." I considered several of them friends. It was hard, however, not to compare the amazing generosity of the ordinary folks at the "Daily News" with the actions of the big shots representing the owners of the Cox newspaper chain.

The family that owns the Cox newspaper chain is now worth more than $20 billion. Back in the late 1980s, that family, sitting on its billions, hired a notorious "union busting" law firm from Nashville, Tenn.

I guess that is how a family holds onto its billions and sees the pile grow—by squashing pipsqueaks like Jerry Range.

The first good medical event in a long time had come on July 9. Dr. Casalmir removed the tracheotomy and I was freed from the ventilator. It had been a terrible way to live for those eight months. It was uncomfortable. It was a health hazard, because bacteria collected in the tracheotomy tube. It was just plain misery.

By mid-August, I had increased my time for sitting in the wheelchair in a single period to nearly four hours. The travel time for us to New Philadelphia from Kettering was somewhere between three and one-half to four hours.

We left Dayton on a brutally hot August 17, 1990. Four hours later, we pulled into the scraggly backyard of our new home. Tom was completing a new ramp up to the back porch.

Mary Rose and Christopher had seen the house several weeks earlier, and her reports were dismal. I understood why when I entered the house. There was one small bathroom next to the back door. The kitchen needed a new refrigerator and other repairs. The floor sagged in many places. There was a small front room, a former office that Jeannie and I used as a bedroom. There were three rooms upstairs. The house needed a thorough dusting.

There was no air conditioning. Some of the screens needed to be replaced.

That night the skies in eastern Ohio opened up and rain did not stop for a week. There were holes in the kitchen roof, and water was cascading down through the kitchen cupboards. Jeannie was near tears, and I was slipping back into depression.

She had to pick up Christopher after eighth-grade football practice several days later in Dover. It was pouring rain, and Christopher climbed into the van caked in mud. There is nothing a young football player likes more than playing in mud. He looked over at his mother and said, "You don't seem happy, Mom. You don't like it here, do you?"

"Christopher," Jeannie said, "give me a chance. It has been raining forever, water is gushing out of the kitchen cupboards, and your father is becoming depressed again. And everyone else in the family is at each other's throat."

"Well," the muddy warrior said, "it just doesn't get any better than this."

Perspective is everything.

There were six of us living in the old wood-frame house. Mickie soon would join us after leaving her job as a dental assistant in Dayton.

Jerry Jr. had been enrolled in the University of Toledo. After I got deathly ill, he ignored Toledo. When I got out of the hospital and back to our Kettering home, I called the university and asked if he were still enrolled. He was, and I was told that based on my new future earnings, he qualified for financial aid covering the entire cost. In his first quarter there, he posted a

3.4 grade point average. That was far better than his high school grades.

Then he dropped out of the University of Toledo and returned to Dayton. He said he was in love with a girl he had met in June. She was a bimbo. He was living above a dentist's office, and working as a fry cook in a rundown nightclub on Kettering's seedy west side. He was attending Sinclair Community College in downtown Dayton. He was taking fewer and fewer courses.

I called him from New Philadelphia and said, "Jerry, you are getting further and further from your goal of a college education. Why not come up to New Philadelphia and get a job. Then enroll in the Kent State branch campus here." For once, he took my advice. He worked for two days in a pallet factory. The place was filled with ex-cons and other equally unsavory characters.

So he went to every business at the local indoor mall. He first got a job frying fish for Arthur Treacher. Finally, he became part of the security team at JC Penney.

Mary Rose seemed determined to make my life a living hell. In the spring of '91, I called her friend's father and asked if she could stay at their home while going to high school at Archbishop Alter. He readily agreed.

"Mary Rose," I said, "we cannot go on like this tearing each other apart. So here's the deal. I have talked to Colleen's father in Kettering and you are welcome to live at their place while going to high school at Alter. Your other choice is to begin treating your mother and me decently. Make your choice. I need your answer one week from today."

A week later, Mary Rose came to me and said, "Dad, I'm not going to go back to Alter. Things will be different. It just won't be the same. So I will stay, and try to make things easier on you and on Mom."

There was no miraculous overnight change in her. However, as the weeks and months went by, changes for the better occurred.

Not so subtle changes clobbered me. First I got scabies. Jeannie had to shave my head and cover my entire body with some foul-smelling ointment. Next, I developed a severe case of facial impetigo as well as a fungal infection on my face. For nearly a month, my face was wrapped in bandages covered with two medications.

"So this is how Job got his start," I told myself.

End of Chapter 13

CHAPTER 14

"It is NOTHING that I fear."

Only Jeannie and I knew that I was a dramatically different person, physically and emotionally, when we pulled into the backyard of my brother's rental house in New Philadelphia on that sticky-hot Aug. 17, 1990.

Stripped to the waist, covered in sawdust and sweat, my brother Tom was just finishing the building of a long ramp up to the back door.

"Welcome to beautiful New Philly," Tom yelled as Christopher, 14, was unloading me from the van. "I have a hospital bed set up in the front room."

"Oh shit," I said to myself as I rolled off the hydraulic ramp, "with him shouting like a barker in a cheap carnival, we could sell tickets to the neighbors looking on."

"Jer," Tom said, "this is Dick your neighbor sitting on his porch steps to the left. And over there is your other neighbor—wave!"

"Tom, I can't even lift up my hand from the control of this electric wheelchair, let alone lift my arm to wave to someone." I said.

Dick seemed to understand the situation, and he shouted, "If you need help, don't be afraid to call for it."

On the other hand, the other neighbor had an expression on his face that I had seen hundreds of times before: "Why are you here? Are you contagious?" He quickly vanished into his house covered with thick, gnarled ivy vines.

"Tom, I am at the end of my rope physically. I've got to lie down to rest my lungs," I said. "You and Jerry Jr. stand on either side of the ramp to keep me from driving off, while Christopher helps me keep this thing going straight up the ramp. It's a nice ramp, Tom, and it will be great with handrails. But I really don't have any strength left to talk."

Jeannie and I went into the room where the hospital bed was set up. There were tears in her eyes as she surveyed the room. It actually had a door to the small front porch, which we soon barricaded with a chest of drawers. The house was not air-conditioned. It was about 90 degrees outside and just a few degrees less inside.

"I'll get the fans from the van," she said.

Jerry Jr. was already on his way to take care of that task for his broken-hearted mother.

We were all bathed in sweat. Our nerves were as taut as piano strings.

My mother planned far in advance, and I soon created a crisis in the extended family's planning for Christmas. The families of my two brothers, my father and mother, and a niece and her husband had been participating every year in what seemed to me to be an odd festivity called the "progressive dinner."

It just seemed a damned silly idea: at each house, the holiday revelers would eat one course in the holiday meal. Then everyone would put on their coats, scarves, gloves, and hats and troop over to the next house for course No. 2; the same for course No. 3, and then onward to the final house for dessert. Early in November, my mother told Jeannie that the rest of the family expected us to join the "progressive dinner."

"Now, let me try to get this straight," I said to Jeannie. "You're saying that my relatives go from house to house in 25-degree weather eating one course at each house?"

"Yes," she said.

"You're kidding, aren't you?" I asked.

"No," she said, "apparently they have been doing this for many years and they think it is a fun thing to do on Christmas Eve. Frankly, Jerry, I have my doubts."

"Well," I said, "I would use a much stronger word than 'doubts,' but I don't want to swear. Don't they understand how difficult it is to load me into the car and to unload me; to get me in and out of cold-weather gear? And my body has difficulty in adjusting from severe cold to a heated home. Somebody must have been nipping at spiced-up eggnog to come up with this cockamamie idea."

I let it be known clearly that I would not be taking part in the "progressive dinner" tradition. Whereupon, my mother said that if Jerry was not taking part in the "progressive dinner," then she would not participate.

A firestorm of epic proportions erupted over several weeks with the phone lines buzzing. Eventually, they had their "progressive dinner" with some of my older children taking part. They simply were not willing or able to understand that I was different than I had been before my most recent near-death experience.

As far as my relatives could see, I had always been in a wheelchair, and I was in one now. So how was I any different?

Well, I was a Catholic who could not make the Sign of the Cross.

I could not feed myself, wash myself, and take care of my toileting needs (I had to use a bedpan, and that onerous duty fell to Jeannie).

I could not shampoo my hair by myself, nor could I shave myself. I could not dress myself. I could not position myself at the desk.

I needed someone to arrange for me books, a newspaper, a glass of water or soft drink, and the remote "clicker" for viewing cable television.

I needed help to blow my nose.

I could not scratch my nose, or any other place on my body. That inability would become an almost maddening deficiency.

I needed help positioning myself in my wheelchair, and I could not shift positions in the wheelchair. That meant that over a 12— or 14-hour span of time an enormous amount of sweat built up. That added to the problem of itching.

Unlike people with spinal cord injuries, post-polios like myself have tactile ability; that is, we can feel whatever is touching us or whatever we are touching. And we itch like hell, because sweat collects in many places during 12-14 hours of sitting in a wheelchair.

The loss of all the movement was a reduction in freedom.

My energy level was far lower than it had been before the second crippling.

I could tell people these things, but the spoken word shatters on an uncomprehending mind like a crystal champagne glass thrown into a fireplace on New Year's Eve.

Leaving Kettering had drained us all.

Jeannie made a large sign with the face of a clown whose mouth was turned down in a frown. There was a big tear falling from his eye. In cartoon style, he was saying, "Goodbye." Jeannie hung it up in the lobby of St. Charles Church in Kettering.

"Mostly," Jeannie said back then, "leaving this house will be so difficult. I'm going to miss all of the beautiful trees sheltering us. You won't have the wraparound ramp. It was wonderful the way the contractor made it come out of the kitchen area and take you in a short arc around to the shade of the trees behind the house."

The neighborhood in New Philadelphia was drab—call it "a working-class neighborhood"—compared to the upscale one we had left in Kettering. A few days after we had moved in, Peter was out riding his bike. A young man of about 20 or so with long unkempt hair came up to him at the corner and pulled out a knife. He said, "C'mere, little boy, lemme show you a fun game." Peter ran home. I didn't find out about the incident until the next day.

Thankfully, there were no more incidents. But it put me even more on edge. I thought, "My God, what have I brought my kids to?"

To give our kids something to rally around, we "adopted" Tuscarawas Central Catholic's varsity football and basketball teams. Peter, 8, became a ball boy for the football Saints.

Going to football and basketball games and getting to church once a week was about all I could manage. I was constantly short of breath, and when I became tired, I was susceptible to a panic attack.

My heart would race. I would call Jeannie. She would get me to breathe deeply and exhale slowly. After a few minutes, the attack would subside.

Something that would not go away was our steadily worsening money situation. When we married, we consciously decided that if Jeannie got pregnant, she would stay home with the children. Luckily, I made enough money in both Cleveland and in Dayton to keep us afloat. We carried a heavy load of debt, but we still got by.

For the first time in our married life, we were a charity case.

The pastor of Sacred Heart Church, Father Ed Keck, gave us hundreds of dollars in cash many times in our first three years in New Philadelphia. Tom often brought groceries.

I was trying to support eight people on what we got from Social Security and a small supplemental insurance check. Our income was barely more than $1,200 a month.

Out of that came $372 the third day of each month as rent on the house. There was a standing joke in the family that it must be the third of the month if Aunt Karen was knocking on the door.

That left a little more than $900 to pay bills, buy groceries, and to get the kids the things they needed for school. By the middle of each month, we were out of cash. By December of 1991, we had a list of at least ten creditors with whom we were seriously in arrears. There was no way we would be able to clear those bills.

Normally, Jeannie goes right to sleep the moment she hits the bed. One night, in the dark in our "bedroom," I listened as she oh-so-softly cried.

"Honey," I said in the dark, "come here." She came over to the hospital bed and lay down beside me. "Jerry, it's only the 10th of the month, and we have no more money for groceries. Seven people called me today demanding that their bills be paid. I know you think that I'm terribly disorganized, and that's the biggest part of our money problem. But there's simply not enough money coming in."

She lay with her head on my right shoulder while holding onto my right arm so that it would stay around her neck. She gently cried herself to sleep on my arm.

"My God," I said to myself, "after all that I have put her through both by my being poisoned and re-paralyzed and most of all by my stupidity and callous treatment, she still trusts in me and looks to me for strength."

We filed for Chapter 11 bankruptcy in federal court in Canton. It was humiliating and degrading. The bankruptcy judge treated us with open contempt. It seemed as if he was spitting his words at the people who appeared before him.

He gave all of our creditors until May of 1992 to file claims seeking whatever could be recovered. In May, we attended the second hearing. There was a humorous moment. We had signed a note for Jerry Jr. when he bought a used Yugo in Kettering before my hospitalization.

The dealership was a General Motors distributor. The financing came through GMAC.

We owed about $900 on the damn thing. No one would buy it. We were delighted when GM had someone haul it away. Jeannie and I felt a little sorry for the young lower-level functionary whom GM had sent to reclaim its used Yugo.

A lawyer friend of my father's recommended a firm in Cleveland that had three cases involving poisoning by amino acid capsules. Judges all over the country were ordering the consolidation of the cases. Ours was given to the firm of Weisman, Goldberg, and Weisman. It had 50 cases.

It was the kind of prestigious firm that did not need to advertise on TV. Attorney Eric Kennedy was to direct our case.

Kennedy said to us, "I'm not going to kid you. This might be a tough, long fight. But I think you do have a good case."

"We're not the kind of firm that will be holding your hand all the time. We will only call you when we have something important to tell you. If you think you have the strength and the will to fight, I am more than prepared to fight for you. What do you say?"

Kennedy had the pent-up energy of an idling bulldozer, and the eagerness for combat of a gung-ho Marine.

"Everything that I had worked for since age 11 has been destroyed," I told him. "Believe me, I'm ready to fight. Where do I sign?"

A reporter for the local daily, the "Times-Reporter," had heard of my "plight." After several of her requests, I gave her an interview. After the interview, she asked if I had ever wanted to write a column. I told her that it had been one of my goals in the newspaper business.

Shortly afterward, her editor offered me a weekly column at $20 a column to run in Monday's editions.

Jeannie put two stacks of books about 18 inches apart and then I had her put the keyboard on top of the books.

Jeannie stuck an unsharpened pencil into plastic devices that someone had given us. They accommodated the pencil through two holes.

Jeannie took white surgical tape and wound it around the end of the plastic device. I was able to grasp the end of the plastic device firmly between my front teeth and type.

The tape would become gooey and gummy after awhile. So there were frequent repairs. After five or six hours of jackhammer typing by holding a stick in my mouth, my front teeth ached.

Apparently, I struck a nerve in the five or six counties serviced by the "Times-Reporter." In my Monday columns, I attacked the changes in our country's basic moral values and traditional folkways.

I soon became the Rush Limbaugh of the Tuscarawas River Valley. I became especially popular in Mennonite/Amish areas.

I was asked to be a board member of the county board of mental retardation.

Despite my new activities, the prophecy of the nurses in the Rehab Unit back at St. E.'s in Dayton was coming true. Jeannie and I were beginning to tear at one another. Familiarity does indeed breed contempt. We were together too much.

One night, before she went off to bed in the room to my right, we began shouting at one another. All day long, I had been griping about anything that came to mind. Why did it take so long for her to pick up the younger kids at school? Why couldn't she get dinner on the table earlier? Why couldn't she keep the central room where I sat less cluttered?

"You always criticize," she yelled, quite uncharacteristically. "You never say something nice about the things I do for you! You are always negative! This has been hard on everybody! I know what you have been through, but I have been there with you. You never seem to recognize that."

"Yeah, goddam it, but you . . ."

At that moment, Peter, 8, came down the stairs. He was trembling, although it was not a cold night.

"Dad, please don't yell at Mom. She's had a really tough day. She was telling us when we were coming home in the van that we should be extra nice, because you were having a bad day again. Dad, you have a lot of bad days. Can't you do something about it so that Mom won't always be afraid of you?"

Peter always has had the ability to talk to me honestly and directly. It is almost as if he can reach right into my heart, diagnose the problem and massage the hurt.

Jeannie and I talked the next day and agreed that I had to go for psychiatric counseling again. She was right: the kids couldn't talk to me, because I was so irritable.

"There's constant tension in the house," Jeannie said. "You are so down all the time. It's dragging us all down.

A psychiatrist in Canton prescribed a daily dosage of an antidepressant drug, and adjusted the dosage until we reached the suitable amount. That got me the sleep that I needed.

Getting the correct dosage of the antidepressant did not have me turning cartwheels of joy, but it put a "floor" under my emotional strength. He also prescribed an anti-anxiety agent that worked. And, he listened to me in half-hour sessions.

He sent me to a psychologist in Massillon for further counseling.

That psychologist helped me to understand that long ago Jerry vs. the world had changed to Jerry, Jeannie, and the kids vs. the world.

"Look, from what you have told me, you were always the center of attention," he told me. "The kids in high school rallied around you as the symbol of St. Joe High School.

"Even in college where there were more than 100 handicapped students, you said you were the only cripple in the journalism curriculum. When you went to work, you were the only cripple in the newsroom in Cleveland. The same was true in Dayton.

"So when you married and began having children, you did not easily give up the spotlight to your wife or to your children."

The psychologist helped me to understand that trying to stay in the spotlight was one way I tried to manipulate life. He got me to step away from myself and see how ludicrous it was for someone totally crippled trying to control the flow of life. He got me to stop looking at clocks. It was a liberating time.

I had been raised to think that by chopping up life into segments of time, I could control life.

With six children, that kind of thinking was impossible. When one of the parents was severely crippled, it was absurd. For more than 20 years, I often had made Jeannie miserable by my belief that I could control life. I finally started to let go of the reins. It eased the tension.

"God does not care if we are late for mass," I said one Sunday. "It's the effort that counts." Jeannie thought I was being sarcastic as usual. But she began to understand that I was serious about not caring about controlling time.

I still had the tendency to bite off more than I could chew. I agreed to serve on the search committee for a new superintendent for the county board of MR/DD. That took from early September until December.

At the same time, Coach Teynor's grown children came to me and asked me if I would organize a tribute banquet for him. He had announced that the 1993 season would be his last.

"I have never done anything remotely close to this," I told his children, daughters Cindy and Terry (since deceased), and son Tim.

"We know how close our father and you have been over the years," Tim said. "Dad would not want anyone else organizing it."

One way of dealing with the boredom and resulting frustration that grows larger as the ability to move shrinks is to immerse oneself in energy-sapping pursuits.

A huge amount of my time is spent doing nothing. I have a great fear of nothing. I mean I fear NOTHING. I fear long empty periods of time when I cannot reach for the book I would like to read, turn the page of a newspaper, or get hold of the TV "clicker" just to surf the news/information channels.

It has been 48 years since I was paralyzed the first time by polio, and 15 years ago by a prescribed drug.

It would not be an exaggeration to say that in those 48 years with their double dose of paralysis that an accumulated 20 years of that time were spent doing nothing—nothing while sitting, nothing while lying in a bed, nothing while waiting for a caregiver to find time to help me, nothing while sitting in a car waiting for my wife to finish grocery shopping, or nothing because I might be hesitant to ask for another bit of physical assistance on the heels of help given maybe 5 or 10 minutes before.

I am not a thinker of deep thoughts. I have never had instruction in how to meditate deeply. I am a muser. My thinking during periods of boredom is much like my education—a mile wide and an inch deep. So I skip from one subject to another, but I never get immersed very deeply in any mental pursuit.

I do think about upcoming events in which I am going to interact with other people, and I invent dialogue that I might use. It rarely plays out as I imagine it.

I am not a great fan of television. For most of the decade of the '60s, I did not own a television. I would be a poor contestant on a game show like "Jeopardy," because I simply do not pay much attention to network television with its mindless sitcoms and their laugh tracks. Also, while I like movies, it is difficult to get to them. I do rent movies, particularly when one of my college-age children is home on vacation.

I do watch baseball, and college football on television.

I would like to do a lot more reading, but I cannot physically manipulate a paperback book. They simply will not stay open for someone with one hand, and in my case an almost unusable hand at that.

If I want to read, it must be from hardback books. But $30 for a book is incredibly expensive for someone who is $50,000 in debt, excluding the mortgage. When I do get a new hardback book, I must have someone "break" it for me.

Someone must break the spine of the book in many places so that it will lie open on my desk. But even breaking the spine of a book does not guarantee that it will lie open, or that stubborn pages will not fall back upon the page I am reading.

There is a bit of Walter Mitty in me. At times, I am flying in a B-17 in a raid over Nazi Germany. I am the turret gunner swinging in a 360-degree arc searching for Messerschmitts to blow out of the sky with my twin 50-caliber machine guns.

Or I might be a Marine fighting with my mates to keep control of crucial Henderson airfield on Guadalcanal in the early days of the Pacific fighting in World War II.

Sometimes, I get far into the future and I am a navigator/gunner armed with photon torpedoes. We are patrolling a chunk of space only 900,000 miles across. Occasionally, I'll say to my pilot, "I'm going up top for a look-see." Upon my vocal command, my seat rises straight up into a pressurized bubble atop the spaceship. I radio the nearest controller only 250,000 miles away asking for sightings of alien bogeys. The position of one is radioed back. Away go the photon torpedoes! Scratch one bogey!

I play those little mind games part of the time, but the lion's share of the boredom that fills much of my life is spent hopping from one mental subject to the next.

At the same time that I agreed to more psychiatric counseling, I told Jeannie, "As long as I can push the buttons on the phone using my mouthstick, I will be fine here at home. I want you to volunteer at Sacred Heart to get away from me for a while. You need to talk to other women. Every woman needs that."

She became a regular volunteer at Sacred Heart School. Later she was volunteering regularly at Central Catholic High School.

Jeannie went to mass every Tuesday at 8 a.m. and then stayed for adoration of the Blessed Sacrament (consecrated hosts that Catholics believe are the body of Christ) in the open tabernacle. She also has doctors' appointments in the mornings.

When I get her up at 3 a.m. to put me to bed, I remind her to flip me over on my back before she leaves for church. Otherwise, the aching in my flexed knees and on my left shoulder, which has no muscle padding, will wake me up far too early and it will be a long while before I get relief.

I tell her to use the bed controls to get me to the sitting position with the telephone under my right fingers. Often I can go back to sleep. If not, I can stare out the window at the 40-foot-high fir trees across the road, the cardinals, the blue jays, the rabbits, the squirrels, the chipmunks and anything else that moves. It is likely that in an emergency, I can hit the speaker button on the phone and then hit the programmed "911" button.

During the summer when Peter is home from college, he puts me to bed at 3 or 4 in the morning. He is a night owl like his father. If Jeannie is going to be in Cleveland helping our daughter Mary Rose with our new grandson, I must remember to remind Peter to leave me on my back so that I do not wake up too early due to aching joints.

Patrick goes to work in the summer at Central Catholic at 8 a.m. Once Peter gets to sleep, he is nearly impossible to wake up. No matter how loud I shout, it will take at least an hour to wake him in his basement bedroom. So I have to be sure, given the day, that someone will turn me onto my back before I awaken.

Every day I wake up frustrated.

I do not want to die, but I would like to be shed of this useless body.

I believe in miracles. But I think it is abundantly clear that in my case there will be no physical miracles. First of all, I would have to have the miracle of muscle replacement. All of the muscles in my left arm long ago atrophied. In other words, there are no muscles in my left arm or hand.

After the second paralysis, all the muscles in my upper right arm atrophied. There is some muscle movement in my forearm and in my hand. I do not have an opposable thumb, however. Also, there is no muscle fiber under my right rump. After an hour of riding in the car, my right leg aches like an infected tooth being hit with ice water.

In fact, considering all that has happened to my body and mind, it could be said that it is a miracle that I am still alive, and that I am still functioning more or less intelligently.

But the frustration is always there.

I cannot throw it off in a game of catch with one of my sons. I cannot walk it off. I cannot run it off. I cannot swim it off. I cannot toss it in an arc and see it disappear through the twine below a basketball hoop. I cannot golf it off. I cannot blast it in a volley across a tennis net. I cannot go to a firing range and shoot it off. I cannot see it disappear beneath the surface of a lake as I cast it off.

I cannot even drum my fingers on the top of my desk to rid myself of some frustration.

I simply must accept it, internalize it, and deal with the problems it brings. Boredom, frustration, and the resulting pain of often severe daily headaches and occasional gastrointestinal problems are my cellmates. Sometimes even painkillers do not drive away the pain. That is the law that I live by. I do not like these kinds of laws and the conditions they create, but I have no choice but to accept them.

I cannot create anything with my hands. I cannot drive with my hands. I cannot pick up a golf club. I cannot pick up my grandson, Nicholas Patrick Smolak.

I feel as if I am going through life, but I am not part of life. I am an observer of life, not a participant. I would like to drive a boat on Lake Erie. I would love to cruise around Erie Bay on a summer's day with the mid-summer sun skipping golden coins across the water.

The only thing that I can do is string together bunches of words, but words are written in the sand. Unless one is a truly gifted writer, his words are quickly washed away. Rarely are they saved. As a writer, I am a Clydesdale in the Kentucky Derby.

Severe cripples live desperate lonely lives on barren islands in a desperate sea filled with other desperate people.

With my civil lawsuit, I had managed to enter briefly the parallel world that people who can walk inhabit.

Because of a number of coincidences, my case moved along quickly.

Eric Kennedy, my tenacious lead lawyer, set a date late in 1992 for the "interrogatories," the grueling cross-examination by the enemy lawyers.

My oldest son, Jerry Jr.; daughter Mary Rose, Jeannie and I drove up to Cleveland for the crucial showdown.

The first session began about 10 a.m. It lasted nearly four hours. The three enemy lawyers took turns interrogating me and hammering away at two points. First, they tried to prove that we had discounted other factors. They were trying to reduce the overall effect of the 11-month ingestion of the doctor-prescribed amino acid tablets.

Second, they took turns trying to blur the line between the crippled Jerry Range before I took the tablets and the crippled and seemingly unchanged Jerry Range after Dec. 20, 1989—the day on which I entered St. Elizabeth Medical Center.

After 3 1/2 hours, Kennedy called a timeout. He wanted to give me a break and some advice.

"You're talking too much," Kennedy said to me. "Just give them 'yes' or 'no' answers. Don't volunteer information."

"Oh, Christ, Eric, I knew I would screw it up," I said.

"No, no, you're doing fine—just limit your answers," he said giving me a strong pat on the back. "Really, you're doing fine; now go back in there and give them hell!"

"Can I go have Jerry Jr. empty the urine bag first?" I asked.

"Hell, yes, and take one for me," the feisty little infighter said.

Jerry Jr. and I returned to the conference room in a few minutes. The grueling, repetitive questioning resumed. Hour after hour, the enemy lawyers pounded away at the ever-narrowing theme: it was not the amino acid tablets that had crippled me the second time, they claimed, and I was no different now than before I had taken the tablets.

Finally, after four more hours of questioning, I lost it.

"You sons of bitches! You took from me everything that I had worked for since Aug. 15, 1955! You took from me my ability to feed myself, my ability to wash myself, my ability to get in and out of my wheelchair!

"You bastards took away something even I can't put a price tag on. You added huge chunks of boredom and frustration to my life.

"Worse even—far worse!—You took away my ability to hug my children. Goddam it, you made it impossible for me to sleep with my wife!

"Never again will I be able to roll by myself onto my left side and wrap what was once my good right arm around my wife and cradle her warmly against me. What the hell else do you want from me?"

"You bastards, you . . ."

I began to sob violently. My heart was thundering in my chest, and the hot, stinging tears of bitterness were pouring down my face.

Jerry Jr. gave me a bear hug from behind, and said, "Easy, Dad, easy, we love you." Mary Rose wrapped her thin arms around me and cried along with me.

Kennedy jumped up and physically interposed himself between the enemy lawyers and me.

"This session is over, gentlemen. My client has had enough."

I was crimson-faced with the emotion of the moment, but also because of my humiliating performance. I was ashamed of losing my self-control.

In the lobby, Jeannie was getting me into my winter coat. Kennedy came up and said, "You did great, Jerry, just great!"

"Eric," I said, "don't patronize me. I made a fool of myself in there."

Kennedy came around directly in front of me, leaned both of his arms against the arms of my wheelchair and said in a harsh, fighting-mode voice: "When I say something, by God, I mean it. And I'm telling you that you did great."

"But my breakdown in there, my crying . . ."

Kennedy cut me off. He said slowly, deliberately, and fiercely: "They—do—not—want—to—mess—around—with—you—in—court!"

End of Chapter 14

CHAPTER 15

"I Love You, Dad."

Kennedy, the leader of the legal team fighting for me, called me around noon on a day early in November 1992. "I've got good news for you," he said.

"I sure as heck can use some of that," I said.

"The other side wants to settle, and we are here in Columbus in the offices of the arbitration firm that they're using," he said. "They have several proposals. I need you to sign off on some of these."

We were on the same wavelength, so agreement came quickly. "Stay near a phone. I'll be getting back to you later today."

Around 5:30 p.m., Kennedy called on his cellular phone. He said that he and the rest of the legal team was ten miles north of Columbus.

"We have an agreement in principle awaiting your approval." He spelled out the details of the agreement. I was using a speakerphone. Jeannie was at my side listening. We agreed that Kennedy had hammered out a good deal.

"Eric, we have a deal," I said.

"I thought you would like it," he said. "I'll set up a time for you and Jeannie to come to Cleveland to sign the releases, which protect the defendant from further litigation by you."

"Eric," I said as I began to choke up, "I'm glad our paths crossed."

"Likewise, buddy," he said, "likewise. I'll be in touch." In late

February 1993, we went to Cleveland and signed the releases. On the wall of Kennedy's office was a framed copy of an essay about a day at old Cleveland Municipal Stadium. I had won a contest sponsored by the "Akron Beacon Journal." Jeannie had it framed. We had given it to him.

"I want to make something absolutely clear," Kennedy said. "Never divulge the terms of the settlement. That could put in jeopardy the entire agreement."

With Jeannie's whole-hearted approval, I took a large chunk of money and paid off debts that my father had taken on after his retirement so that he and my mother could stay afloat. Eliminating his debts would allow him to pay off medical bills he owed after his quadruple-bypass heart surgery.

A few years earlier, I had come across a copy of my retired father's tax return. His tiny pension and Social Security payments were shocking.

"I just can't let my father worry about unpaid bills or making the monthly payment on the re-mortgage," I told Jeannie.

Peter was then in the fifth grade at Sacred Heart School in New Philadelphia, and Patrick was in the third grade. Both of them would be playing basketball over a total of six years in the gym on top of the church's social hall. I did not look forward to being pulled up the 12 steps every time they would be playing in a basketball game.

Father Ed Keck, the pastor, was in a wheelchair. He had been paralyzed from the waist down in a traffic accident.

"Jerry, from where I sit," he said with tongue firmly planted in cheek, "your plan for a long ramp with a wrought-iron railing and a flat space for resting midway up and a new door at the top is a no-brainer." So we built a 95-foot brick and cement ramp.

Later that year, the old coach announced at the beginning of the '93 football season that it would be his final campaign after 36 seasons.

"Jerry," he said, "most people think it's because I'm 67. Actually, the damn diabetes is screwing up my legs. The pain gets so bad I sometimes forget the play we're running in practice."

In August, when I heard that the new principal, a young man with an ego the size of New York State, had crossed swords with the Coach on the practice field, I went to the principal thinking that he did not understand how respected Coach Teynor was among Ohio coaches.

"Maybe it would be useful for you to have some background on Coach Teynor," I said.

The principal launched into a half-hour story of the glorious things the teams he had coached at a private school in New England had done.

"Well, thanks a lot for your time. We certainly have accomplished a lot here today," I said after the self-serving dissertation. The sarcasm was lost on him.

Coach Teynor's final team, with my sophomore son Christopher breaking into the defensive lineup, went 7-0. Then we lost on a Saturday night to a league rival 7-6 on a missed extra point by our senior kicker.

On Sunday night, normally a time when the Coach and his small staff would be studying game tapes, he called me and said that seven sets of parents representing eight senior players (there were twin linemen) had called him and demanded that he come to school in the afternoon.

"When I got in there," he said, "they asked me to quit immediately."

"Was the principal there?" I asked.

"Yeah," he said, "but he didn't take part in the so-called discussion. Who needs this kind of treatment? Maybe I should quit right now."

"Coach, back in the 1958 season, when you were squeezing two victories out of a team that didn't give a damn about anything, you taught me never to quit. I know that your legs are giving you hell, but please don't give in to that group and don't give up."

He stayed on. The team went on to win the league title while posting an 8-3 record. It made the Ohio playoffs. In any sense, it was a successful season.

I had called the principal at home.

"Did you allow the school to be used for that kangaroo court where the whining senior parents demanded that Coach Teynor resign?"

"I did not take part in any of the discussion," he said.

"I don't give a damn if you sucked your thumb," I said. "You should not have allowed the school to be used for the senseless attack on a fine and decent man!"

After that, I was determined to do everything I could to make Coach Teynor's testimonial dinner something special. Gerry Faust, former coach at Notre Dame and at the time the coach at the University of Akron, agreed to be the keynote speaker.

I quietly set up a new-car fund. I called more than 600 people asking for a donation to the fund and urging them to attend the banquet. With only a week to go, we had only 140 reservations.

"Maybe prayer will help," Jeannie said. She prayed, and it poured reservations. More than 350 people crammed into the cafeteria the night of the banquet.

The local Chevrolet dealer was preparing a black Chevy Corsica with gold trim (the school's colors), including a small fleur de lis on both sides of the car.

During the banquet, we passed the hat and collected another $1,100.

Faust showed up right on time. When my meal was placed in front of me, Faust said, "Do you want me to feed you?" Just like that: no hesitation, just, "Do you want me to feed you?"

I said, "Forget the vegetables."

"Oh, no, you have to eat your vegetables; they're good for you."

"I don't like vegetables."

"Eat them anyway," he said. He made me clean everything off my plate, including the damn vegetables. After the meal, six of Coach Teynor's former players from earlier eras spoke. My daughter Mary Rose, former trainer, represented the "modern" era.

Mary Rose alluded to the Coach's tongue-in-cheek criticisms of her choice in boyfriends while in high school. She said, "Coach, you will be happy to know that I now am dating a suitable boy—

one of your former players who soon will be in medical school, Michael Smolak."

John Hayes, a former journalism professor at Temple University, recalled that when he entered high school at old Dover St. Joe, he was about 6-foot-3, and weighed about 200 pounds. He did not want to play football.

"However," he said, "anyone that big had to play football at St. Joe or his budding manhood would be placed in question."

Then Faust spoke. He talked softly and movingly of his trip to Lourdes, France, site of the apparition of the Blessed Virgin Mary.

"I sat down next to a middle-aged guy who said he was from Ireland. He told me that he had advanced cancer and had only a few months to live.

"The guy was holding a rosary," Faust said. "I asked him if he were praying for a cure."

"The guy said, 'No, I've had a good life, and my kids are grown. I'm praying for those kids over there.'

"He pointed to a group of severely crippled kids," Faust said. There were very few dry eyes in the cafeteria.

Then I got the microphone. My son Peter, 11, and the Coach's son Tim had walked over to my brother's house nearby after Tim had brought his father to the banquet. Tim drove his father's new car to the school and parked it right outside the cafeteria door.

"Coach," I said, "what goes around in life comes around. With that thought in mind, my son Peter—your ball boy for three years—is now going to walk down to you and give you this key ring." The Coach looked perplexed.

"On this key ring, Coach, you'll find a key that will open up the door and another key that will start your brand new Chevrolet Corsica, which is parked right outside the door to your left. Enjoy it, Coach. It's a gift from all your boys."

Tim got up and said, "Jerry, I think my father would like to look at his new car." (Later Tim told me that he wanted to give his father time to regain his composure).

A minute or two later, the coach came back in and said in that old familiar gruff voice, "Who put snow on my new car?" Several inches had piled up during the banquet.

Only one other time in my life had things gone so well—on my wedding day and night.

Unfortunately, the coach's diabetic condition worsened considerably in the next 20 months. The blood flow to his legs slowed to a trickle. One day he called me and said, "Jerry, I can't take this any longer. I can't sleep. I can't eat. All I do is think about the pain. What the hell am I going to do?"

I struggled to find words that could ease his pain. There were none, but I knew from experience that having another human being hear of his pain was of some small comfort. Soon, he had most of one leg amputated. Still the pain persisted in the other leg. Part of that leg was removed. Eventually, he lapsed into a semi-comatose state.

Jeannie and I visited the coach in a Canton hospital. He was lucid, and heavy doses of painkillers gave him peace.

Jeannie, teary-eyed, hugged him. The Coach and I squeezed each other's hands as Jeannie lifted mine to reach his. I found reassurance in that great paw, as I had back in 1958 when we first met.

He died with his family members around him. They asked me to eulogize him at his funeral mass.

"The coach," I said, "helped a skinny crippled kid develop a positive self-image of himself by making that crippled kid feel useful in a good cause. During his first season we played a road game in mud so thick that players could barely run. We lost 6-4. Our record was 0-4.

"As my father was trying to get me across the field after the game, the coach came over and pulled on the wheelchair while Dad pushed. The coach said, 'Well, we'll just have to try again next week.'

"That," I said, "summed up the Coach's approach to life: 'Keep trying.'"

Then I thanked his widow and his children for sharing their husband and father with me and many others.

In the fall of 1994 I slammed head-on into my 50th birthday. It was time for a prostate exam. Our family doctor came to the house and gave me a physical. I mentioned that I had been having tightness in my chest.

"We'd better schedule a stress test for you in Canton," he said. "A cardiologist will inject you with a medicine that will simulate stressful conditions for your heart," he said.

The uncomfortable test indicated some sort of blockage. That made me an immediate candidate for an exploratory heart catheterization. The jamming of a plastic shunt into an artery close to my groin was less than fun. Then a thin fiber-optic line went down the shunt, and up to my heart. I got to watch it all on overhead TV.

It was cold in the procedure room, and I was nearly naked. I was nervous. The doctor asked, "What do you think of the procedure?"

"Well, it's better than a sharp stick in the eye, and preferable to a car wreck, but on the whole I'd rather be in Philadelphia—the old one," I said borrowing the old W. C. Fields line.

He did not seem amused. The artery over the front of the heart was totally blocked. They inserted the "balloon" to clear a path through the gunk in the artery.

I had eaten my last McDonald's quarter-pounder.

I began eating raw cauliflower like popcorn. Raw broccoli was on my plate three or four times a week. No more steak, no more gravy, no more biscuits, no more rich desserts, no more bacon, no more deep-fried anything, few eggs, and no more cheese. Oh, Lord, a life without cheese!

I also began ingesting five more pills a day—one for blood pressure, another for keeping the heart muscle strong, yet another for getting fluids out of my body, and two potassium pills to counteract the one for getting fluids out of my body.

Combined with the medications for fighting depression and anxiety, my pill count went to 11 a day. With a $500 deductible and a 20 percent co-pay, my yearly drug bill climbed to more than $6,000.

Of course I could not get the pills to my mouth by myself. It was five more strings that the Lilliputians, who can only be seen by severe cripples like me, employed to bind me to a life of minutiae.

After the settlement of the lawsuit, we bought a house in a neighborhood called Schoenbrunn. Dad drove over several times a week.

"Dad is losing far too much weight," Jeannie said in the summer of 1995. "He takes protein supplements, and eats a high-protein diet. But he keeps wasting away." His body was inexorably shutting itself down.

If I were not yet up in my wheelchair for the day, he would sit by my hospital bed and we would talk baseball. I often thought, "I never played catch with my father. When I could walk as a kid back in Erie, he was too busy. I'll never get that chance."

Years later, my second son, Christopher, put it in perspective after I had mentioned the same thing about the two of us. "Dad, I always wanted to play catch with you, but I thought of our talking about baseball as the equivalent of our playing catch."

It bothered me that I had never said to my father, "I love you."

"Well," he said one afternoon, "Mom soon will be done with her bridge club. I better be getting along. You know what a stickler she is for my being on time." He put on his windbreaker, and pulled on his baseball-type hat.

Just as he got to the door of my room, I said, "Dad?"

"What is it, Jer?" he said.

"I . . . I love you, Dad," I said with great difficulty.

His eyes glistened as he said, "I love you, too, Jer."

We never parted after that without telling each other, "I love you." Each time it was easier to say. It is one thing to know that you love another person. It is another thing to know that the other person knows of your love.

The world changes forever when one person tells another for the first time, and later for the last time, "I love you."

Dad's life was crumbling. One day, he told Jeannie and me, "Yesterday, I started out driving on the east side of North Wooster Avenue, and the next thing I knew I was sitting in the car several blocks west of Wooster Avenue. I have no idea how I got there. What the hell is happening? I'm scared."

"Don't let them put me in a nursing home," he said. "I don't want to end up in one of those damned 'warehouses'."

Eventually, he was no longer able to walk well, or even to get up out of a chair. Mom, 76, tried as hard and as long as she could to give him the help he needed. Jeannie wanted to take him into our home, but I told her that the burden on her would have been overwhelming. So he was put into a nursing home.

"One day when I walked into his room at the nursing home," Jeannie said, "Dad looked at me sadly and said, 'Don't you love me anymore?'

"It was like someone was crushing my heart. I said, 'Oh, Dad, of course I love you!'"

On a warm September Sunday, Tom rolled Dad in a wheelchair the two blocks from the nursing home to Dad's home of 40 years. We sat on the screened-in patio where he had presided over so many cookouts.

"Okay, who wants steak and who wants hamburger? Speak now or forever hold your peace," he would shout from just beyond the screened door as he tended the grill.

During the meal as he shoveled more steak onto your plate he would ask, "Better have some more, we'll only throw it out. Is it okay? Are you sure? We can always cook some more."

When the eating was over and on the table were platters and bowls that held remnants of steak, sweet corn, fried squash, bean casseroles, scalloped potatoes, and garden salads, he invariably would say, "Some people could make a meal out of that."

I was jolted back to reality when my emaciated father sitting in a wheelchair asked, "Do I have to go back?" Soon after that, he lifted his trembling hand and looked at an imaginary watch.

"They'll be serving dinner soon. We better get back before they lock the doors," he said.

Younger brother Jim called on the morning of Sept. 29, 1996, and said, "Dad died about 6 a.m. They are calling it a massive heart attack."

"Dad didn't die of a heart attack," I told Jeannie. "He died of a broken heart. He wanted out of there, and this was his way of getting out."

In my eulogy for Dad, I reminded my mother and my brothers of that night 18 years before when he was honored at a retirement party in a restored hotel in the tourist hamlet of Zoar.

A few months before he retired, he had made the biggest sale of his long life as a salesman. He sold more than a million firebrick to Union Carbide, which has a plant on the Ohio River.

Dad often said about his favorite baseball player Ted Williams that he admired Williams' on-the-field play, but he admired even more the fact that Williams retired when he was still at the top of his game.

At the retirement banquet of my Dad, I said, "That is exactly the way that my father is leaving the sales game. He is leaving it at the top of his game. He is a class act. He has been a class act all his life."

I ended my eulogy by saying, "That is how we should remember Dad—as a class act."

My father had been banged around by the American economy harder than baseballs in batting practice, but he never lost faith in the American dream he had been given: hard work will get you a better life, and will assure your children of an even better life.

He believed in that so implicitly that he was sure his badly crippled son could succeed.

We buried Dad in a Catholic cemetery. He was never confirmed in the church. For decades, he had attended mass with my mother. He never formally became Catholic, but the parish priest offered him communion before his death, and he took it. The priest also gave him the last rites.

If being a Catholic means caring for other people, and I believe that is a vital part of being a Catholic, then Dad was a Catholic.

Dad once sold to a young Amish couple a new stove fueled by a tank of propane gas. He helped the technician install it. I remember him describing how excited the young woman's pink face looked under her distinctive white "Dixie-cup" bonnet.

Several days later, the crestfallen couple came back in their buggy to the bottled gas outlet that Dad managed. The young Amish bridegroom said, "The elders say that we cannot keep it."

My father could have said, "A deal is a deal. I can't take it back." But he did take it back.

An old high school friend of mine home from college shoplifted a few items from a discount store. They were worth $1.29. The manager wanted to prosecute in mayor's court. Dad convinced the mayor that a good life might be badly crippled if the young man had a conviction on his record.

Dad talked the manager into dropping the charges. My friend never got an arrest record, and he went on to a highly successful career in the world of finance.

Every so often, I think of calling Dad to talk about baseball—the equivalent of "playing catch," as Christopher had described it.

Then I remember Dad is gone, my eyes mist over, and I say quietly, "I love you, Dad."

End of Chapter 15

CHAPTER 16

"The Light Awaits"

Dad would have enjoyed his granddaughter's wedding.

Mary Rose, our second daughter, married Michael Smolak in September 1998. She had just gotten her degree in special education, and was teaching in a suburb of Dayton. Her bridegroom was in his final year at Wright State University Medical School near Dayton.

When she came into the back of the church where I was waiting, I looked at the stunningly attractive, slim young woman in white and wondered: "Is this the pudgy little girl who in her little burgundy velvet dress with the frilly white lace collar used to lean over my leg and ask: 'Daddy, when are you going to walk?'"

Her sister Michelle, or "Mickie," as she prefers it, was fussing over her younger sister, making sure that everything was in its place.

Mickie has been an anchor for the younger children in every crisis since she was a teenager. It was Mickie who kept the other five children from spinning off into unrecoverable orbits during the darkest days of my near-death crisis from late December 1989 to late January 1990.

It was Mickie who saw that the younger boys got their homework done, who made supper, who washed dishes, who did the laundry, and who made sure that the younger boys got to bed on time.

It was also Mickie who gave her mother a much-needed humor break. On one of the infrequent nights that Jeannie came home from the hospital, Mickie said, "Come on, Mom, we're going to the movies."

"Oh, Mickie," Jeannie said, "I couldn't sit through a movie right now."

Mickie insisted until Jeannie gave in. She took Jeannie to see "Steel Magnolias."

In the penultimate scene at a moment of great tragedy, the character played by Olivia Dukakis urges the grieving mother played by Sally Fields to "punch her lights out," referring to Shirley McLean's character. All the characters burst into laughter, and on come the much-needed tears of both joy and sadness.

"All the fear, all the sadness, and all the worry came flooding out of me," Jeannie said. "I laughed so hard that I cried. It was a tremendous release for me. I don't know what inspired Mickie to take me to that show, but it was just what the doctor ordered."

In the church vestibule, Mickie deemed Mary Rose ready for her marriage Mass.

The music also indicated it was time to go down the aisle.

"Showtime!" I said.

"Are you ready, Mary Rose?" I asked.

"Yes, Dad," she said.

"Mary Rose," I said, "I will always love you."

"Dad," she said, "don't say anymore or you will make me cry and ruin my makeup."

"Well, then," I said, "let's get the show on the road." She held onto the handle grip of my electric wheelchair, and we marched to the front.

On Dec. 15, 2000, Nicholas Patrick Smolak came outside his mother's womb for a look-see, and decided to stay.

The labor was long and arduous. During the process, Mary Rose developed a dire blood infection. We briefly thought Nicholas might lose his mother. But my kids are fighters. Mary Rose battled and won.

Eighteen months before Nicholas arrived, Christopher, son No. 2, became the third of my six children to graduate from college.

He was a communications major at the University of Dayton. He and a young woman were given the job of composing a litany of "We owe you" messages to recite to the 6,000 parents, other relatives, and friends in attendance in UD Arena.

They reeled off things like: "We owe you a lifetime of thanks," or, "We owe you four years of 'care' packages," or, "We owe you four years of worrying."

Finally, Christopher stepped to the microphone and in a loud, clear tone said, "We owe you 80 thousand dollars."

The mighty roar that rang out from the assemblage of 6,000 sent the Richter scale off the charts.

I was enormously proud of Christopher.

Mickie is the organizer and anchor of the family.

Jerry Jr. is our man of iron, and our soft-speaking loyalist and family peacemaker. Standing nearly six feet tall and weighing well over 210 pounds, he is married to a tiny little redhead named Karen. She is a lovable 4-foot-11, 90-pound dynamo.

Christopher, son No. 2, is the family comedian. He does a fabulous Sean Connery impersonation.

Peter, about 160 pounds, is the family blonde. He explains to people who ask about his appearance that he was "struck by lightning," or at more mischievous times, says, "The mailman and Mom were very friendly." In addition to being our resident wit, he is fast becoming the family intellectual.

Dark-skinned Patrick, at 245 pounds, is peripatetic. In high school, he was co-captain of the football team, president of his class, a Eucharistic minister, a mass acolyte, and has been a member of the Sacred Heart Parish council for a number of years. In college at John Carroll, he has become active in student government, serves as a tour guide for prospective students, and organizes religious retreats.

There is no lack of courage in Patrick's heart. When he was a freshman on the Central Catholic football team, he was the largest player. His position on offense was center and interior lineman on defense. As a freshman he snapped the ball to his brother Peter, a junior quarterback.

We were losing 25-0 to Strasburg, Central's hated archrival. We scored late in the final quarter. As our players came off the field to get instructions for the kickoff, Patrick lay writhing in pain on the goal line. Peter heard his younger brother and rushed to him. He had nerve damage in his left shoulder. We also learned that he had congenitally fused vertebrae. Several local doctors told us that he should not play football.

Patrick was crushed. He begged us to see a specialist; one of the local doctors recommended an orthopedic specialist in Akron. We went to see him. After looking at the x-rays, the doctor came into the examining room, hopped up onto the table with Patrick and asked, "How important is football to you?" Patrick said, "It's everything to me."

The doctor said, "Have you considered joining the golf team?" I thought for moment that Patrick might strangle the doctor. The doctor said, "If you were my son, I would not let you play football. However, if you can regain all of your strength in your left arm, then you can play football. However, another injury like this will end your football career."

Jeannie urged me to tell Patrick that he could not play football. I said, "I simply cannot take that away from him. I will keep close watch on him every game, especially watching for 'stingers' which indicate damage to the nerves."

He played his final three years in high school. Unbeknownst to his mother, he did have many "stingers." None of them were detectable by his mother however. He played through a lot of pain. He was truly heroic, besides being one heck of a football player—a true profile in courage.

Our six kids shout and fuss at one another, but they always go their separate ways as friends. They all are enormously loyal to their mother and father.

Christopher recently told me, "I went to a party after we beat Garaway High in football my senior year, and one of their players was there. He'd had too much beer. He said to me, 'How do your parents do it (have intercourse)?' He thought that was a funny question."

"What did you do?" I asked.

"I taught him a very painful lesson in etiquette," Christopher, a solid 180 pounds, said.

Fourteen months after Christopher graduated from the University of Dayton, his younger brother Peter, then 18, entered the freshman class at John Carroll University, a Jesuit-run liberal arts college in University Heights, Ohio, in the hills east of Cleveland.

The picture-perfect campus looks like it could be the movie set for "Andy Hardy Goes to College."

Political correctness does not abide in Catholic universities. Even the Pope's ideas must battle in the marketplace of ideas on Catholic campuses. There is no free ride for a one-track train of thought as one might find on an Ivy League campus. In other words, among the Jesuits who run John Carroll University there are liberals, there are centrists and there are conservatives.

I abhor political correctness. That is one of the reasons that I refer to myself as a "cripple." I refuse to be bound by other people's claims on the language. Part of my vehement objection to legalized abortion is that I have a vested interest in the preservation of all human life, no matter how insignificant. The polls consistently tell us that mine is a minority opinion. To hell with the polls.

Peter fell in love with learning. He is wrestling with the kinds of ideas that I am. His mind is alive and expanding. He is his own man as a 22-year-old senior.

When we were returning Peter, then a freshman, to campus on the Sunday after spring vacation at John Carroll, my mind went back to one particular football game when he was quarterback. He started 19 of 20 games in his junior and senior years. He missed one game as a result of the concussion in his junior year.

We played perennial state powers like Newark Catholic, Villa Angela/St. Joseph of Cleveland, and other behemoths. But the worst physical beating he took was against the Fighting Irish of Bellaire St. John's, a "river team." The city of Bellaire is on the Ohio River near Steubenville and Wheeling, W.Va. Football in the upper Ohio River Valley is a take-no-prisoners affair.

As we traveled northward toward University Heights, I mentally replayed that vicious, brutal game. Peter was sacked 12 times, and was hit at least as many times after he had thrown a pass. It was if he were continually slamming into thick numbered rocks covered with green, the opponents' color.

As the game wore on, he was limping visibly, and was leaning over after each play trying to fill his lungs with air. When the final whistle mercifully blew, he hobbled into the line of his players to shake the hands of the winners.

I could catch snatches of what Peter's coach was saying in the team meeting on the field: " . . . beaten on the scoreboard . . . big hearts . . . thanks for the effort."

Peter came walking gingerly off the field toward me where I sat behind the end zone. Down by his leg, he was dangling his golden helmet. There were streaks of green—the opponent's helmet color—on his helmet and the rest of his uniform. His entire body sagged. I would not have been surprised if he had said, "Dad, I want to quit."

I love football, but I would not have argued.

"Dad," he said after leaning over and giving me a hug, "now I know how Custer felt just before the final arrow got him."

I was astonished. "How can this kid keep taking this kind of pounding?" I said to no one in particular as he limped off toward the bus.

"Where does his physical and mental courage come from? Every week the scoreboard says we are a loser, but every week Peter walks off this football field or some other field one hell of a winner."

"I have been blessed with great kids," I mused as we neared the John Carroll campus.

"In another year," I told myself, "when Patrick goes off to college Jeannie and I will be back where we started, just us two. This time we won't be the starry-eyed young lovers we were when we married. There won't often be that magical aura when we touched.

"But somehow we must find a way to turn the negative energy of our enforced intimacy back into the delight we knew as first-time lovers."

That past summer we sat on the observation deck of Beach No. 7, the "handicapped beach" on Presque Isle State Park on the peninsula protecting Erie, Pa., Bay. The number of interracial couples surprised me. I watched as a young black man languidly rubbed suntan lotion over the golden-colored back of a young Caucasian woman.

We will not be a color-blind society before my death, but we are making progress.

Neither will I see in my lifetime a society that is totally open to crippled people, but we are making progress.

It was twilight when we got Peter back to campus.

Eighteen months before, he had been savagely thrown to the turf time and time again in nine ignominious varsity football losses.

Each time, he had risen slowly from the field of battle. He had fought the good fight, and he had kept the faith in himself and in his cause. He had shaken off the pain and humiliation, had kept his eyes on the greater prize, eventually to find himself at John Carroll University.

He opened my door, leaned into the car, and gave me a hug. "I love you, Dad," he said.

"I love you more than you know, Peter," I said. Then he lightly bounded up the steps to his dormitory door held ajar by a wedge of wood.

All around us in the parking lot, other young people were saying goodbye to their fathers.

"This is why we fathers are willing, if need be, to march through the valley of the shadow of death for our children," I said to myself.

"We fight whatever, whenever, and wherever life commands, so that young people like Peter can enter a promising future."

Framed in the doorway light, Peter gave the thumbs-up signal, flashed his winning smile, turned, and stepped into a future aglow with hope.

The End.

EPILOGUE

It probably would benefit a reader of this epilogue to know that my story was not intended as an inspiring narrative of how a cripple succeeds against all odds. If this story inspires someone, so much the better.

First and foremost, this true story was intended to be a narrative that hopefully would "grab" people's interest and hold it to the end. I thought that there had been enough drama, struggle, pain and moments of joy in my life to be worth the retelling.

I wanted someone to direct me in the attempt, someone skilled in the use of the English language. I wanted that person to be hard on me so that the best story would emerge.

In addition, I wanted someone who did not share my view of the world—religion, cultural viewpoint, political opinions and so forth. I am a Roman Catholic with a conservative view of culture in America.

For my "writing coach" I chose Wes Hills, a longtime friend and skilled reporter at the Dayton (Ohio) Daily News, a paper of about 230,000 circulation.

Hills is an atheist and member of the Hemlock Society. I am pro-life; he is pro-choice. I am a critic of the ACLU; he is a dues-paying member of that group.

I began writing my story in early spring 2001.

Hills' primary command was: "I want you to open a vein and bleed." I tried to do that. When I strayed, Hills was scathing in his criticism until I got it right.

*   *   *

There have been three significant events worth the telling in my life in the 2 1/2 years since I finished writing my autobiography.

First, three years ago I became a grandfather, as my daughter Mary Rose gave birth to the dancing fool, a.k.a. my grandson Nicholas, as he has become known in my columns.

In fact, I have done so many columns on his development and, stretching a point sometimes on his "dancing" (swinging and swaying for instance in front of the television while one of his favorite cartoon movies plays), that many readers have come up to me and asked, "How is the dancing fool?"

He is a great All-American kid just full of piss and vinegar. He has been a great tonic for what has ailed me.

Our oldest child, Michelle, 33, showed remarkable strength of character—and more than a little grit—when she was diagnosed with a brain tumor in the spring of 2002.

I always told my kids that information is power, and Michelle (she prefers "Mickie") obviously took that lesson to heart. She works in the hospitalization insurance business, so she is conversant with many different kinds of medical plans, with hospital administrators and with doctors, including their reputations.

She was first diagnosed at Aultman Hospital in Canton, Ohio by a neurosurgeon who did all of his operating work there. The city of Canton is bisected by I-77 and is only 60 miles south of Cleveland via I-77. So she called the world-renowned Cleveland Clinic, and was examined by a neurosurgeon there.

Both of the surgeons suggested surgery; the difference was that the neurosurgeon in Canton said that there was no reason to operate immediately. Unsatisfied with that, she sent her x-rays to a neurosurgeon in New York City, who had links with New York University. He examined the x-rays as well as results from MRIs that were done on her.

The New York neurosurgeon agreed with his Cleveland counterpart that immediate surgery was the better choice. So, armed with information that empowered her to make a reasonable decision, she chose to have the operation soon after in Cleveland.

She came through with flying colors. The surgeon said that all of the tumor had been removed. At a follow-up exam, she asked him if the tumor was cancerous. His reply was, "By definition, all brain tumors are cancerous. It is not a question of *IF* your tumor returns," he said, "it is a question of *WHEN*."

Michelle has had three routine examinations—if an examination for a brain tumor can be called "routine"—since her surgery. So far so good: there has been no reoccurrence or discernible growth of the tumor.

There is one interesting sidelight to the story. Early after her surgery, she went to a seminar given by the Cleveland Clinic on people who had brain surgeries done at the Clinic. All the people in the audience identified themselves and where they lived.

Out of an audience of about 150, 19 people said they were residents of Tiffin, Ohio. Tiffin, a community of about 17,000 people, is in the northwest part of the state, about 40 miles southeast of Toledo. Obviously, there is something strange afoot in Tiffin, Ohio.

Michelle has, to put it mildly, a rather assertive personality. Others might call it an in-your-face kind of personality. She loves her younger siblings enormously, after overcoming her disgust at not being an only child.

Anyway, whenever our kids get together at holidays or for other family gatherings, some how Michelle seems to bring the conversation around to her brain surgery. It has become a family joke: "IT ALWAYS GETS BACK TO YOUR BRAIN SURGERY," the others now say in unison when she begins to talk of it.

She is a young woman with a seemingly impenetrable outer shell, but on the inside is a heart capable of great love and deep compassion. Jeannie is especially happy now because Michelle has returned to the church and once again is a practicing Catholic.

*   *   *

Back in the summer of 1996, I had developed some blocked arteries which were reopened by the use of the angioplasty technique (the "balloon method") in which a tiny fiber-optic wire with a small balloon-like device at the end is run up into the heart clearing up the blockages where too much plaque has collected and has slowed down the movement of blood into and out of the heart.

The blockages had been discovered by my family physician, Dr. John Burnham, M.D. He was doing a routine prostate exam in my home when I mentioned that I felt that there was some kind of "constriction" in my chest.

He immediately phoned 911. I was taken to Union Hospital in Dover, was sedated and monitored. Twenty-four hours later I found myself in the rather cold arterial catheterization unit of Canton's Mercy Medical Center 30 miles up the road.

Several blockages were cleared, and eight hours later I was on my way home. The doctor doing the procedure asked me how it felt. I said, "Well, it is certainly better than a sharp stick in the eye and certainly better than a car wreck (I owe those metaphors to a great copy editor in Dayton, Bob Brim)."

The heart doctor did not seem to appreciate the humor.

In the summer of 2002, Jack Burnham again was doing a prostate exam at my home. He asked me how my heart felt. "Well, there has been some tightening around the heart area," I said innocuously. He immediately picked up the phone and called 911 again.

Twenty-four hours later I was once again in the "cath" unit at Mercy Medical. Again, one artery was cleaned out. Actually, doctors can only reduce the blockage to about 25 percent for fear of poking a hole in the artery. A few hours later I was back home.

However, in February 2003 the telltale signs were back again. So we went to the hospital thinking that the artery over the back of the heart—that one had been difficult to get at—probably needed some more work.

When a surgeon named Dr. Antonios Chryssos told me that I

needed open-heart surgery, I felt as if I had been punched in the face.

Nurses on the coronary care unit later told us that Chryssos had pioneered a new procedure in this region. The medical acronym is "midcap," which stands for "minimally invasive direct cardio-arterial procedure."

During the procedure, a small incision about four inches long is made above the left breast. The ribs are spread apart with a protractor. If the surgeon can reach the area of the heart that needs work, he can anesthetize that area, and taking an artery from the mammary region, work on the heart while it is still beating.

We were told if he could not reach the area that needed treatment, he would resort to breaking open the sternum and putting me on a heart-lung machine.

I did not want to undergo surgery. I said to Jeannie, "Sweetheart, I have climbed too many mountains. I just cannot climb another one." When my six children, my son-in-law Dr. Michael Smolak, and my daughter-in-law Karen, herself a profile in courage, heard of that, they surrounded my bed in Mercy Medical.

They reminded me of what I had always told them—keep fighting regardless of the score. And they reminded me of the plaques.

When my son Peter, 22, was a 17-year-old senior quarterback at Tuscarawas Central Catholic High School, 19 young men including Peter and his sophomore brother Patrick, then 15, reported for preseason football practice for former Coach John Zucal.

For the final game of the season, only 16 were physically able to suit up against state powerhouse Newark Catholic. Newark Catholic annihilated the Saints by 60 points.

All of the Saints' nine losses were lopsided; 47-0, 52-0, 58-7 were commonplace.

I always had told my children, all of whom played high school athletics, to put everything they had into the game. "Never quit," I told them over and over. I have always believed in what some would call a stale cliche: "If you leave everything on the playing field, then you will be a winner regardless of what the scoreboard says."

I had 19 plaques made. On them was this inscription from legendary sportswriter Grantland Rice: "When the One Great Scorer comes to write against your name—He marks—not that you won or lost—but how you played the game."

Coach Zucal allowed me to give each of the heroic 19 a plaque at the sports banquet.

When I was thinking of what I was most thankful for during Thanksgiving week 2003, the real reason behind the plaques came to mind.

So, when the family gathered to celebrate Thanksgiving nine months after my surgery and a prayer was offered before the meal to the loving God who just won't let go of me, I said in my heart: "Thank you, God, for allowing me to struggle throughout this precious life that you have loaned to me."

The most annoying part of the surgery for me was doctors and nurses swarming about the operating table sticking needles into me trying to get intravenous "ports" started. With my under-developed arms and legs, I am a notoriously "bad stick."

When I awoke from the anesthesia, the nurses made me sit up in bed. The pain was so intense that I was convinced someone was stabbing me in the chest. Dr. Chryssos believes in a minimum of painkiller, so as not to prolong the recovery.

But the pain was so overwhelming, and probably owing in part to my being disoriented, my heart rate shot up to over 150 beats per minute.

And I was having a severe panic attack, one of the things that have bedeviled me throughout adulthood. I could not communicate because of the breathing tubes down my throat. One of the worried-looking nurses asked me if it would help me to calm down if she were to bring my wife Jeannie to my room. I nodded vigorously in the affirmative.

Jeannie came. Just the sight of her helped calm me. Her voice, that always happy voice, flowed over me like I was like being dipped in the soothing 88-degree water at Warm Springs, Ga., where I had begun my rehabilitation from polio 48 years before. Within 15 minutes, my heart rate had slowed to under 110.

Jeannie is a life force; everything and everyone who comes in contact with her prospers by the experience. Flowers, shrubbery, dogs, stray cats, rabbits, squirrels and chipmunks, friends, children and one particular husband flourish in her sunny smile. Even at age 57, she remains the lovely, modest, innocent young woman of 23 who was given to me at the altar of St. Rose of Lima Church in Cleveland in 1969.

I cannot imagine life without this gentle, giving, loving woman.